COMPETITION CAR
ELECTRICS

COMPETITION CAR
ELECTRICS

Jon Lawes

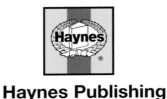

Haynes Publishing

First published in July 2006

A catalogue record for this book is available from the British Library

ISBN 1 84425 302 3

Library of Congress catalog card no. 2005935267

Published by Haynes Publishing, Sparkford,
Yeovil, Somerset BA22 7JJ, UK

Tel: 01963 442030 Fax: 01963 440001
Int. tel: +44 1963 442030 Int. fax: +44 1963 440001
E-mail: sales@haynes.co.uk
Website: www.haynes.co.uk

Haynes North America, Inc.,
861 Lawrence Drive, Newbury Park,
California 91320, USA

Printed and bound in England by J. H. Haynes & Co. Ltd, Sparkford

**Jurisdictions which have strict emission control laws may consider any modifications
to a vehicle to be an infringement of those laws. You are advised to check with the
appropriate body or authority whether your proposed modification complies fully with
the law. The author and publishers accept no liability in this regard.**

**While every effort is taken to ensure the accuracy of the information given in this
book, no liability can be accepted by the author or publishers for any loss, damage or
injury caused by errors in, or omissions from the information given.**

Contents

Introduction

A FRENCH MAGAZINE organised a reliability trial in 1894 in which cars competed to maintain the best performance with the minimum of breakdowns. Soon after this first trial, an offshoot of domestic vehicles appeared which was designed with one purpose in mind: to compete. Before racing cars became high-speed advertising hoardings promoting products to the spectators the budgets were dictated by the depth of pocket of the driver, but as racing has become more commercialised and pockets have become deeper, race engineering has become an industrial discipline on a par with, and sharing a lot of technology with, the aerospace industry.

As reliability has become more of an issue with highly stressed tight tolerance racing machines the quest for a failure-free system has become the holy grail of the race engineer. Many people view the electrical side of the racing car with great distrust, and some of the electricians in the industry do not make much of an effort to dispel the myth that these systems are over complex. A well-designed and maintained electrical system is often the most reliable part of the car, and here, I hope to be able to advise and guide those who wish to understand their vehicle and therefore get the best from it.

Reliability in electrical systems is largely down to good practice during design and construction, and this book is intended to guide you through some of this process. Due to the huge diversity in motorsport I have been unable to cover every discipline, but I am sure that there will be enough advice, information and guidance to provide for a majority of readers. This book caters largely for those who are entering motorsport perhaps for the first time, possibly preparing their first car, or those who want to strip a little of the esoteric jargon away to reveal the common sense lurking beneath.

Acknowledgements

I WOULD LIKE to thank the following for their assistance in compiling this book:

Richard Barfield at STACK Systems
Clive Chapman for his support and valued friendship
Bob Clarke for the motivation and humour along the way
Grayston Engineering Ltd
Steven James at Tony James Component Wiring Ltd
Paul Martin for his photographic skills
Peacemarsh Garage for access to their 'toys'!
Simon Slade for PIAA UK
Simon Crosse, Theunis du Plessis, Terry Lawless, Paul Parker, Elliott Russell and many others for supplying me with excellent photographs
Everyone at Wren Classics
And of course my family for their patience and support.

Chapter 1

Basic principles

IT IS ONLY NATURAL to assume that the readers of this book will come from vastly differing backgrounds, with very different levels of experience with electrical systems. Therefore, this chapter gives an insight into the basics of electrical theory for those who wish to learn some simple principles, while allowing the more experienced reader to skip through with no real detriment to their knowledge. Although not definitive, this introduction provides a useful foundation of knowledge which will be useful for the beginner.

Some simple definitions

To a novice it can be quite unnerving to be swamped with electrical terms which seem to bear little relevance to the bundle of cables they are trying to install. Because of this, I am going to explain some common definitions in a way that can be directly related to the tasks you may carry out on your competition vehicle. This is followed by a more in-depth description for those who require further information.

An *amp* defines how much *current* is flowing in a circuit.
Basically, to compare it to another system on your vehicle, think of it as being the electrical version of fuel flow rate. The higher the amperage, the more current is flowing. The more current that flows, the larger the cables that carry it need to be.
Advanced: An ampere is defined as one Coulomb of current flow per second in a circuit. A Coulomb is equal to flow in the conductor of 6.25 x 10 to the 18th electrons.

A *volt* is the *potential difference* between two points in a circuit, such as the terminals of a battery.
Basically, to compare it with another measurement found on your vehicle, think of voltage as being similar to oil pressure.
Advanced: One volt is equal to the difference between two points in an electrical circuit dissipating one watt of power and carrying one amp of current.

A *watt* tells us how much power is dissipated by a component or circuit.
Basically, to compare it with another measurement on your vehicle, think of wattage as being similar to the horse power required to drive ancillaries.
Advanced: One watt is equal to the power produced by a current of one ampere acting across a potential difference of one volt.

An *ohm* describes how much resistance there is to the flow of current. It is usually signified by the symbol Ω.

Basically, think of an ohm as being similar to friction, providing a resistance to the flow of current.

Advanced: One ohm is equal to the resistance between two points on a conductor when a potential difference of one volt produces a current of one ampere.

Some basic formulae

Above are the most common denominations used in electrics, and as you have already seen from the advanced descriptions, they are quite heavily interlinked. This connection between the different quantities is useful to us, as we can establish unknown quantities in a circuit, for example when trying to find out what gauge cable we need for a wiring loom, by simply taking the quantities we know and applying them to a very simple formula. Don't panic, it's very basic!

V = I x R   Or in other words, Volts = Current multiplied by Resistance.

So if we only know the current draw and resistance of a circuit, we can find out the voltage applied. But what if the Current draw is the variable we are trying to find? The formula rearranges simply into this;

I = V/R   Or, Current = Volts divided by Resistance.

Equally, we might know the voltage and current draw, and wish to calculate the resistance of the circuit or component. This is decided as:

R=V/I   Or, Resistance = Voltage divided by Current.

This set of formulae is known as Ohms Law, and is often set into a triangular pattern to make it easier to remember:

V
I R

By removing the variable you are trying to find, this leaves the figures you know, in a pattern that tells you exactly how you need to manipulate them. If we want to know V for example, we remove it from the triangle, giving us IR, or I x R. If we want to find out I, we remove it from the triangle, leaving V over R, or V divided by R. Thus Ohms Law can be remembered easily using this technique.

The power dissipation of a component is slightly different. This is the amount of power that a component uses during its operation. Sometimes that power is converted into motion, as with an electric motor. Other times it is converted into light or heat, although heat is often a by-product of the main process. If we want to work out the wattage dissipated by a component or circuit we need to multiply volts by amperes. For example, if a circuit is drawing 12V and 5A, the total power dissipation is 60W.

Resistance

Resistance is the amount of opposition a component will put up to the flow of current through it. Everything has a resistance; what varies is just how big that resistance is. If we enlarge the size of the conductor we can flow more current through it as the electricity has more paths to take, just as widening a corridor will allow more people to pass through at any one time. This means that even though one material may be

Some basic switchgear

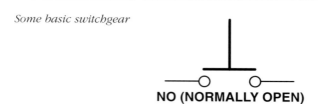

NO (NORMALLY OPEN)

NC (NORMALLY CLOSED)

SPST (SINGLE POLE SINGLE THROW)

SPDT (SINGLE POLE DOUBLE THROW)

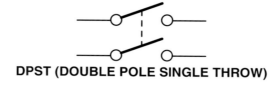

DPST (DOUBLE POLE SINGLE THROW)

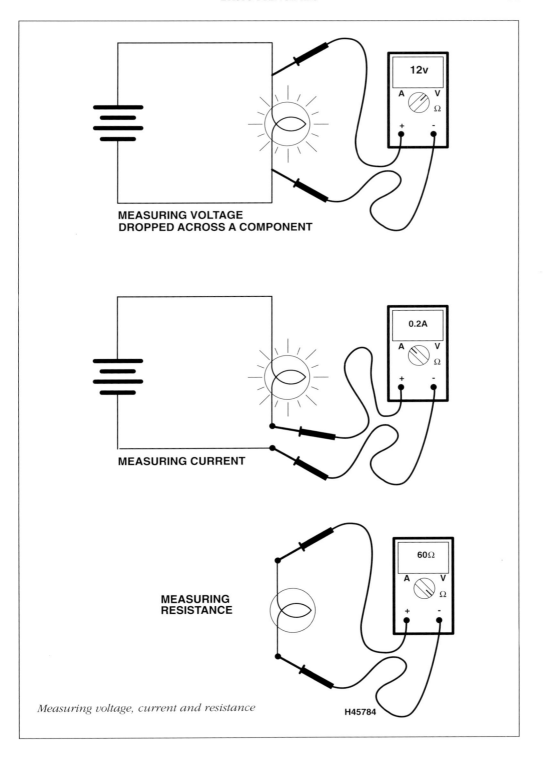

**MEASURING VOLTAGE
DROPPED ACROSS A COMPONENT**

MEASURING CURRENT

**MEASURING
RESISTANCE**

Measuring voltage, current and resistance

H45784

more resistive than another material, we can flow the same current through it by simply making it wider to compensate.

Low-current components in the car, such as interior lights, use quite small cables. This is because the component does not need the wire to be able to allow much current to flow. Compare this with a high-current component such as the starter; the cables are much larger to allow more current to flow. If we used the narrow cable we installed for our interior lights to wire up our starter motor it would not be able to allow enough current through, and the high flow of electricity would be impeded by the resistance of the thin wire. This would in turn generate heat sufficient to melt the cable. Fuses use this principle to act as a weak link in the circuit, providing a narrow conductor through which the entire current draw for the individual circuit must flow. If the current draw rises above that which the cables and fuse can take then the fuse will melt (and blow) before any damage to the component takes place. The more electricity we pass through a resistance the more heat that will be dissipated.

This means that if we pass a current through a resistor the voltage we are left with will be reduced in accordance with Ohms Law. We can use this in a number of ways; the cockpit blower fan in most cars uses a switch with around four settings, 'off', 'one', 'two' and 'three'. When the switch is set to 'off' the circuit is disconnected, preventing current flow. When we set the switch to 'three', or maximum, maximum voltage is presented to the motor, spinning it at top speed. But at settings 'one' and 'two' we place a resistance in series with the motor, reducing the voltage supplied to it. On setting one the resistance is higher than at setting two, meaning the voltage reaching the motor is lower, reducing the speed of the fan.

Dashboard lighting is usually controlled by a device known either as a rheostat, potentiometer or variable resistor. All of these terms refer to the same thing; a resistor that has a variable value depending on where you place a knob or slider. This means that by rotating the knob the resistance value is decreased and the brightness of the dashboard illumination increases. Wiring has an inherent resistance, and the longer the wires connecting a component the lower the voltage will be by the time it reaches it. An example is when people move their batteries to the boot to improve weight distribution they find the engine cranks over more slowly on the starter than it did before.

Series and parallel

The way two or more components are connected is often described using the terms *Series* and *Parallel*. If the components are connected in series it means that current flows into them one after the other, like someone walking through the passageway on a train from carriage to carriage. Components mounted in parallel flow current in the same way that a stream splits into two flows of water, with each path taking a share of the water dependent on its size. Similarly, the electrical components take a share of the current depending on their resistance.

If one component in a series-connected circuit should fail open circuit (in other words, breaking the circuit and stopping current flow) then all the components in that circuit will stop operating. When a component fails open circuit in a parallel-wired circuit the other components should continue to operate. For this reason, headlight systems are wired in parallel, allowing one headlight to continue operating when the other one fails. Therefore, very few components on a vehicle are wired in series. If two identical bulbs or motors are wired in series then each will run at half the power they would if wired in parallel, or on their own. Sometimes this is an advantage, for example, dim-dip resistors are wired in series with the headlights to reduce their output by dissipating some power in the form of heat energy, thus reducing the amount of power available to the bulbs.

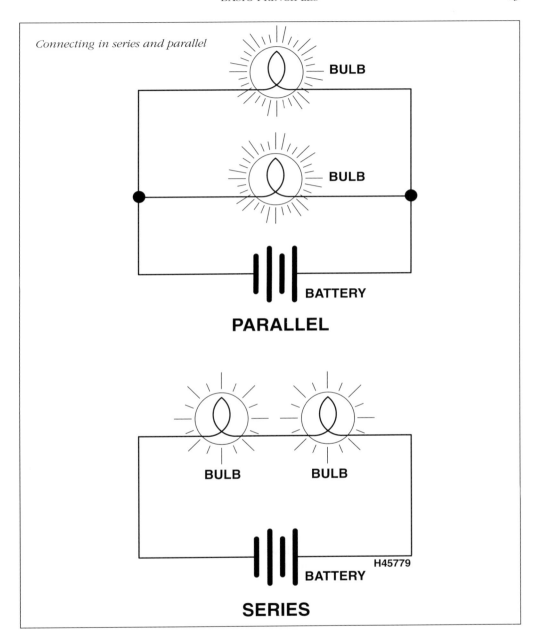

Connecting in series and parallel

BULB

BULB

BATTERY

PARALLEL

BULB   BULB

BATTERY   H45779

SERIES

Creating a circuit

A circuit can be likened to a bucket chain of people standing in a circle. If each person carries a bucket, they can only accept another bucket if they first give the one they are holding to the person on the other side of the one they are being offered. This means that once the buckets are being passed around in a loop, a flow has been achieved. In an electrical circuit the items flowing are electrons rather than buckets while the people passing the buckets equate to the atoms in the conductor. If the loop

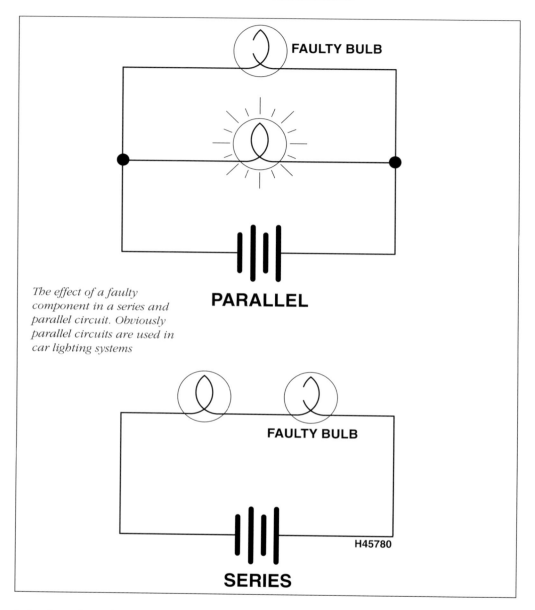

The effect of a faulty component in a series and parallel circuit. Obviously parallel circuits are used in car lighting systems

is broken then there is nowhere to pass a bucket to, so the last person in the loop cannot accept another one. This means that the flow stops virtually instantly. In an electrical circuit we need to keep a loop of current flow to allow it to operate, or the electron flow will stop dead. This basic principle forms the core knowledge needed to build an electrical system.

It is not sufficient to simply create a loop of wire and expect the electrons to flow; we have to create an electromotive force, or EMF. This is the encouragement we need to supply to the electrons to get them to flow around the loop. In vehicle systems this is supplied at 12 volts by the battery and the alternator. As mentioned previously, voltage is a measurement similar to oil pressure, so consider that 24 volts as used on lorries is twice the 'pressure' of the system used on the family car.

Materials in which the electrons flow freely are called conductors, as they conduct (ie allow the passage of) electricity freely. Some typical examples of conductors are copper, carbon and steel. Some materials do not allow their electrons to flow freely, and these are called insulators, as they are capable of insulating two conductors preventing them from flowing current between them. Examples of insulators are rubber, porcelain (as used in power lines to prevent the electricity travelling down the pole), and glass. A few rare (and normally synthetically manufactured) materials sit between these two states, and are called semiconductors.

Semiconductors are manufactured from two different materials layered together, and usually sit in an insulating state, preventing current flow, until a current is applied to a certain point in the layer. The semiconductor allows a heavier current to flow through it (as it has now transformed into a conductor) using the small, applied current as a trigger, just as a small pedal pressure applies great pressure to the brake pads in a servo-assisted braking system. If the trigger current is removed then the heavier current is stopped. This is the operating principle behind a transistor, and semiconductors are seldom seen in anything other than diodes (including light emitting diodes, or LEDs) and transistors. Microchips may contain many thousands of semiconductor junctions, allowing them to take the role of many semiconductor-driven components.

To reiterate, to make a complete circuit we require a 'bucket chain' of atoms carrying electrons. In theory then, every component on our competition vehicle needs a wire going from the battery, via some sort of switch, out of preference, to the component, then returning to the battery to complete the circuit. In practice this technique would be very wasteful, as we have the entire bodywork of the car to act as a conductor. Because of this, on modern cars the negative battery terminal is connected directly to the bodywork, and all components complete their circuit by

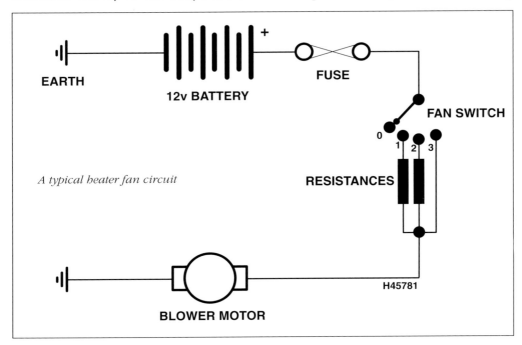

A typical heater fan circuit

going to 'earth'; in other words by also being connected to the bodywork. This system is great for cutting down the amount of wiring we need to carry around, but it does have its disadvantages.

If a positive cable chafes against a metal component on the car until its conductive inner core meets the bodywork a 'dead-short' takes place. This is where all the battery's power is dumped directly between the terminals with no load, and can easily melt cables, cause fires and damage the battery irreparably. Naturally this is something we wish to avoid, and the ways in which this is prevented from happening are detailed in Chapter 5. Normally, the engine has a thick braided strap between the block and the bodywork to carry the current to earth, which the starter motor requires for operation. If this cable is not present the current has to find a different route to earth, and the author has heard rather worrying stories about throttle and clutch cables becoming stiff due to the insulation around them melting. This is because the cables, which were never designed to carry current, inadvertently end up taking the power to earth from the engine block during starting. As they are rather undersized for the task they inevitably heat up and melt the plastic coating that protects them from the elements. Checking the condition of this earth strap should help prevent this from happening to you! Older cars often use positive-earth systems, although this is highly unusual in any vehicle built after 1980. Care must be taken when fitting modern components to these vehicles, as such equipment is exclusively designed to work with negative-earth systems, unless clearly marked otherwise.

The terms amp, ohm and volt, and how they are useful to us have been explained, but how should we measure them? It is important to study this description with care, as connecting an expensive meter incorrectly can result in it being irreparably damaged. Measuring the voltage of a battery can tell us its health, and measuring the voltage drop over a wiring loom (literally the amount of voltage soaked up by the loom due to its inherent resistance) can tell us about the quality of its terminations. In the case of the battery it is simply a matter of selecting VDC (Volts Direct Current) on the multimeter selector, fitting the leads to the common and VDC connectors and carefully touching the leads to the terminals of the battery simultaneously. The red wire must always go to the positive terminal, and the black wire to the negative. This is less important on a digital multimeter, as the LCD displays tend to give just as accurate figures when connected backwards.

Make sure you have found somewhere secure to place the multimeter, especially if the engine is running (which it may be when checking the charging voltage). Also, ensure that the leads can at no time get entangled with moving pulleys or machinery within the engine bay (a caution that also applies to long hair, loose clothing, necklaces etc). During the time you are applying the probes to the battery terminals you can check the voltage displayed, and see if it is in the expected range. To check the volts dropped over a loom you can apply power to it, and then using the same settings applied to the multimeter as we used above, carefully touch each probe to the two opposite ends of the loom (on a single conductor of course). The longer the loom the higher the volts drop is likely to be, but we are hoping for a number as close to zero as possible to ensure that all the connections in the loom are of a good quality.

It is a better technique to measure the resistance of the loom to check it. To measure this, the probes are placed at the same place, but the multimeter is set to ohms, and the probes connected to the common and ohms receptacles on the meter. Again, the lower the value read the better, if an infinitely high value is read either the meter has not been connected properly or there is a break in the loom somewhere.

The next use for the versatile multimeter is the measurement of current draw. You might use this for finding out the rating you need for the cable supplying a

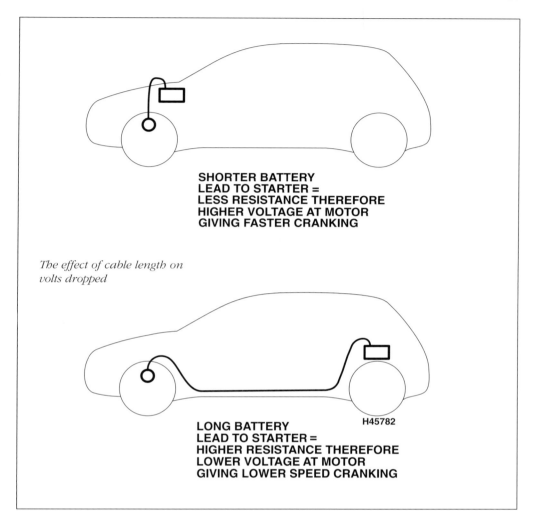

SHORTER BATTERY
LEAD TO STARTER =
LESS RESISTANCE THEREFORE
HIGHER VOLTAGE AT MOTOR
GIVING FASTER CRANKING

The effect of cable length on volts dropped

LONG BATTERY
LEAD TO STARTER =
HIGHER RESISTANCE THEREFORE
LOWER VOLTAGE AT MOTOR
GIVING LOWER SPEED CRANKING

H45782

component on your vehicle. It is important to follow the directions on the multimeter carefully, as damage can occur to the multimeter if you attempt to measure current using the meter connected up incorrectly. Plug the probes into the connectors marked 'common' and 'A' or 'mA', depending on whether you are intending to measure amps or milliamps. If you are unsure which to use, use the Amp setting first to avoid causing damage. If this turns out to be too indelicate for the low currents being measured you can then drop to the mA set-up. Before the probes are in place the meter should be set to A or mA accordingly, and the circuit interrupted between the battery and the component. The multimeter is placed in the circuit in series with the component to be checked.

Be warned that the sort of current drawn by an item such as a starter motor is beyond the scope of the average multimeter, and could cause it damage. For this reason, ammeters fitted to the dashboard of cars are connected in series with virtually all the components on the car with the exception of the starter. When the probes are in place and the meter set to measure the current the power can be applied to the component. Certain components use more power on start up, such as electric heaters and motors, just as accelerating up to speed uses more fuel than maintaining the desired speed once it has been reached. Never change the position of the selector switch while the meter is connected in circuit as you may inadvertently select a setting which causes the meter harm.

Magnetic fields

Whenever a conductor has a current passed through it a field is generated. This field can be used in a number of ways. If the conductor is wound into a coil this affect is boosted, and the magnetic nature of the field generated can be used to pull and push other magnetically attractive objects. In a motor, this electromagnetic effect is used to spin the rotor in much the same way a person would turn a merry-go-round, by grabbing a part of the spinning object, pulling it towards the stationary position, and then changing the force applied to a pushing motion as the part being held passes them. This is the basic principle of the electric motor. If we were to spin the rotor manually by driving it from the crankshaft of our engine the reverse would happen; the spinning rotor would have a current induced upon it by the large stationary

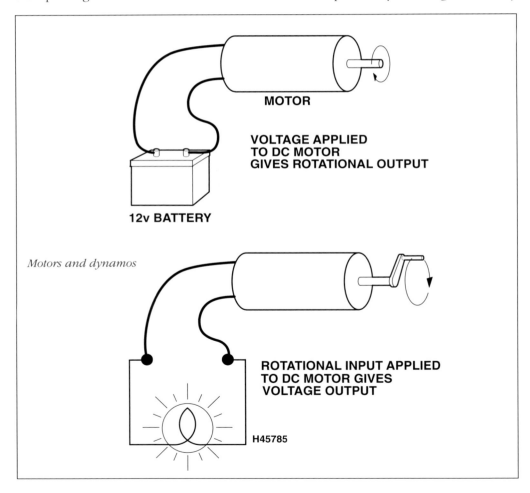

MOTOR

VOLTAGE APPLIED
TO DC MOTOR
GIVES ROTATIONAL OUTPUT

12v BATTERY

Motors and dynamos

ROTATIONAL INPUT APPLIED
TO DC MOTOR GIVES
VOLTAGE OUTPUT

H45785

magnets positioned around it. This is also the principle of the dynamo, the forerunner of the alternator as we know it today.

In the dynamo, the fixed magnets around the outside of the unit are used by the electromagnets in the armature (the rotating part) to provide a field to generate the current. In a motor the field generated by these fixed magnets is used by the armature to give it something to push and pull against. In an alternator the magnets are fixed to the armature and the coils mounted firmly in place, effectively reversing the set-up we had in the dynamo. This is good for reliability, as the big failing with the dynamo is the requirement to take the current from a rapidly spinning rotor. To do this brushes are used, which are carbon blocks designed to rub against a section of the armature called the commutator. Where these conductive brushes rub the electricity flows, which is how the current generated in the coils is fed to the electrical system.

As the electromagnets on an alternator are fixed in place there is no longer any need to use brushes, which means one less part to wear out. The down side is that the current generated is no longer a nice flat 12Vdc; it is instead, a voltage which fluctuates above and below the zero mark at a speed dictated by the speed of the alternator. If this alternating current (ac) is taken and fed through a rectifier (a one-way valve for current) it effectively turns ac into a slightly oscillating dc (direct current). Having to use a rectifier is a small price to pay for the increased power output that a modern alternator provides compared with its dynamo equivalent.

Circuit faults

Now in a perfect world we would not need fuses or multimeters, as faults would never develop in our minimally maintained racing machines. However, in the real world our competition cars are just as fallible as any other device, especially so considering the hard usage they receive. The two main faults that can occur in a basic electrical circuit are detailed here.

Open circuit

As we have seen, a bucket chain of electrons is required to maintain current flow and any place that has this flow interrupted causes a total cessation of current flow in the entire circuit. The circuit could be *opened* by a wire becoming disconnected, a terminal becoming so corroded that it can no longer flow current, or a component in the circuit failing – any number of things can cause an open circuit. Using a multimeter we can discover if an open circuit has occurred by disconnecting the suspect wire and placing the multimeter probes at either end of it. If the multimeter picks up a very low resistance then there is probably not much wrong with the cable. If the resistance is very high or infinite, there is a break somewhere in the cable. The best solution is a total replacement of the failed wire.

Short circuit

On a vehicle using a negatively earthed chassis it would only take an abrasion of a power cable to expose the inner conductor, which would *short* out the battery or component. Literally, a short circuit means that the current has been able to take a short cut instead of the route it was intended to. If one end of the multimeter is connected to the suspect cable, and the other end touches one of the other surrounding conductors (including the chassis of the vehicle) it should be possible to detect a cable which is connected to the cable at fault when it should not be. The best solution is a total replacement of the failed wire, and steps taken to prevent a short from happening again. A short circuit does not mean the current took a physically shorter route; rather it took the route of least resistance. If the current can take a short cut to the battery via a chafe against a bulkhead or similar it will no longer be able to power the chunky component it was intended to supply.

With both these faults the remedy is the same; replace the cable at fault, and take steps to make sure the fault cannot reoccur. Faults like these come down to one thing; poor design and engineering. Put the effort in when constructing your loom and you will discover that irritating problems such as these are much rarer.

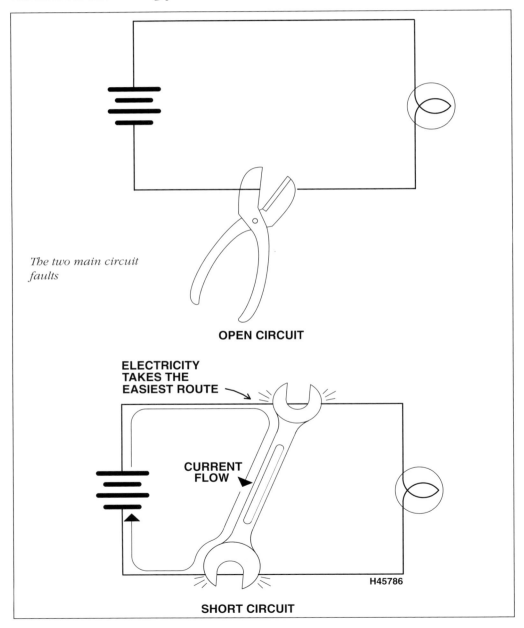

The two main circuit faults

OPEN CIRCUIT

ELECTRICITY TAKES THE EASIEST ROUTE

CURRENT FLOW

H45786

SHORT CIRCUIT

Chapter 2

Selecting cables, connectors and components

WHETHER YOU ARE re-looming your entire car or just fitting a single deviation from the standard system, choosing cables and components correctly is a very important skill to master. For safety, all cabling and components should be easily able to cope with the current and voltage they are expected to draw. However, it is possible to go overboard with this and have cables and components that are oversized and over heavy. It is incredible just how much weight oversized cable can add to a competition car (where weight saving is of vital importance).

The most important thing to consider when selecting cabling is the current it is expected to carry. Certain components are more current hungry than others, and it is often the seemingly simple items which will draw the most current. For example, any heating device, such as a heated rear window, will draw a great deal of current. Motors draw a fair amount and in the case of a starter motor it is enough to warrant an entirely separate wiring system unrelated to the rest of the car. Of course, most motors do not have to turn over an engine, but the greater the work load expected of the motor the more current it will draw.

Another aspect to remember is that just because a device is recorded as drawing 500mA does not mean this will always be the case. A windscreen wiper for instance, will draw a different current depending on the dampness of the screen, speed of the vehicle, state of the mechanical linkage and the presence of any outside interference (such as snow or ice preventing movement). Each of these variable changes could vary the current draw considerably and ideally, a worst-case scenario for each item of equipment should be envisaged. Those with a large budget could even test items on the vehicle under maximum load conditions and measure the current drawn, using an ammeter. The large budget is required because components do not like operating at the top end of their working spectrum, and will more than likely fail, possibly in quite a spectacular and dangerous manner! Consider also a factor known as *duty cycle*.

Whilst a starter motor draws a great deal of current, it does so for a short time only. This means that the cable which supplies it may heat up, but so briefly that damage is unlikely. However, a fuel pump is drawing current for the duration of the vehicle's running time, and therefore the cables supplying it will not have a chance to cool off. The duty cycle refers to the amount of time a component is running, and is usually expressed as a ratio of 'on time' to 'off time'.

Most automotive cabling consists of a copper stranded conductor surrounded by a plastic insulator. The conductive core is made of many strands to allow flexibility and resistance to damage; a solid core is more prone to fracture under inhospitable

conditions. Unless it is claiming some unusual property, such as oxygen-free cable used in stereo installations, larger diameter cable tends to be more expensive than its thinner counterpart. For this reason, motor vehicle manufacturers will use the thinnest cable they can get away with to wire each system. This is the reason cabling needs to be up rated or supplemented when adding extra equipment, such as driving lights.

Also, the way the cable is routed can affect its size and type. A cable packed densely in the centre of a large loom is less able to dissipate heat, and therefore will overheat more quickly than one that is set away from the others. The ability of a cable to carry current can be reduced by as much as 60 per cent by placing it within the centre of a dense loom. Heat dissipation is the primary limiting factor when choosing a cable and it is this ability to disperse heat which gives cables the current ratings they have. The lower the resistance of the cable, the less heat is generated when current is passed through it, due to less impedance to the current flow. This impedance creates a phenomenon known as *volts drop*. This is the loss created by the cable, and can be seen by using an ordinary multimeter. If you measure the voltage of your car at the battery, you may find it is sat around 12.5V say. If you then check the voltage at the tail lamp of the car you might find the figure has dropped by half a volt or even more. This is due to the inherent resistivity of the cable, resistance at the cable joints, resistance at the switch gear, and so forth.

Often, cables will have some form of guideline figure to allow you to assess the volts drop, and better conductivity will normally be reflected in a higher price. As a larger diameter cable has more conductors to flow the current, the volts drop is likely to be lower. Still ever-present though, are the disadvantages of using larger cable: cost, weight, size, flexibility and so on.

Let us try to get an idea of some typical ratings for a fairly high specification PTFE-sheathed cable with a nickel conductor of around a 2A current rating. In this example the conductor is of 30AWG diameter, with seven strands of 0.1mm each. This gives a conductor diameter of 0.3mm, and a conductor area of 0.055mm squared. The rating of this particular example is 377 ohms per kilometre. If this is compared with a cable that is rated at 6A, but is otherwise to the same specification, some difference will be seen. First, whilst the number of conductors remains the same, the diameter of each strand has doubled. This has then doubled the diameter of the entire conductor, and raised the cross-sectional area of the conductor to 0.220mm squared. The AWG has gone up to 24, but most importantly, the resistance has dropped to just 91.2 ohms per kilometre. The cable is identical in its materials and construction method, but with a conductor current rating of twice the original.

The PTFE construction of this example is an excellent compromise of cost and ability. PTFE shows great resistance to oil, hydraulic fluid and fuel and is largely non-flammable, but some formulations can give off toxic fumes when overheated. One of its advantages to the amateur is the number of colour combinations in which it is available, along with its competitive price. However, for most applications the cheaper PVC-coated cable is more than suitable.

For teams with a greater budget, aviation-specification cables are often used. This can be combined with the use of similar specification connectors, which will be discussed later in this chapter. A commonly used cable of this type is Efglas, which consists of nickel-plated copper wire conductors sheathed with a combination of PTFE tapes and a PTFE-impregnated glass material that gives the cable great strength and abrasion

OPPOSITE *Sometimes the sheer quantity of equipment required can mean that good ergonomics are harder to maintain, as this TVR cockpit demonstrates.* (Elliott Russell)

Aircraft-specification connectors in use on an excellently prepared hill-climber. Where these can be afforded they are highly recommended for reliability. (Paul Martin)

resistance. It is available in a screened version (basically a metal overbraid to reduce interference) called Efglasmet, which is ideal for wiring sensors which could be sensitive to outside influence from high-energy ignition devices and such. It has an almost identical ability to carry current as its PTFE counterpart, as the conductor material is basically the same, but the big difference is the material that makes up the insulator.

It may seem of trivial importance at first, but the colour of a cable is not to be dismissed. You may know for certain that the cable running across the bulkhead of your competition vehicle is for the blower motor, but what if later on that cable is joined by five more? Or ten more? Or a bundle of 30 cables, each with a very different task and identical colour? Car alarms are usually supplied with wiring looms entirely made of black wires. Once the loom is fitted and the identifying tags removed it becomes almost impossible to identify what each of the wires does. This is intended to confuse the would-be thief; just as a single-colour wiring loom will confuse you...

Despite this, looms in the aviation industry normally consist of two colours. Most cabling is white, while any which fire explosive devices such as armament or detonate release systems, are coloured red to ensure they are not accidentally disturbed. As an aside, these red cables tend to be placed away from the normal looms to prevent any stray radiated current from other cables initiating the explosive systems they control. The problem of a single-colour loom being harder to trace is overcome by the use of identifying collars placed at intervals along the length of the loom. These collars are printed in an allegedly indelible ink (although sadly, this proves to be often not the case) with a letter and number code that can be related to the wiring diagram for that aircraft. If you intend to use aircraft-specification wiring then this idea would certainly be worth employing, so that with careful planning and preparation the cables can be identified easily when under pressure. Impatient aircrew and impatient racing drivers are a very similar breed!

A cable behind a dashboard has a relatively easy life as it is kept free from corrosive

Clearly marked reminders prevent panic when under stress. (Peacemarsh Garage)

moisture, subjected to minimal heat and free of oils, fuel and grease. Because of this the requirements of an insulating material in these conditions are relatively minor. However, consider that a loom running through an engine bay, often near to components that may carry temperatures of many hundreds of degrees, this will have to have a high degree of tolerance to extremes of temperature, oil saturation and vibration. It is possible to use the same cable as has been used in the rest of the vehicle, but suitably shielded from this harsh environment. Alternatively, a cable of a specification designed to withstand these factors could be used.

Swapping to different cable types within the same loom can have disadvantages however. The most important of these to consider is that wherever there is a cable joint, be it soldered, in-line crimped or a disconnectable plug, there is the inherent likelihood of failure or poor reliability. The fewer terminations a loom has, the greater its dependability will be. Also, wherever there is a joint in two cables, there is an increase in the resistance. Therefore the more terminations in a cable, the more voltage is dropped before the component is supplied with current. If the joint is of a very poor standard the resistance can be quite high and capable of generating much heat. Most wiring fires tend to occur at a termination that has poor conductivity, either due to bad manufacturing processes, corrosion destroying the joint, or impact/tension damage. This is more of an issue where the current to be carried is greater. High current flow coupled with high resistance is the basis of the operation of an electric heater. Unlike poorly made or degraded joints, a heater has a thermostat that kills the power if the temperature gets too high.

Sometimes the type of cable to be used is limited due to the requirements of the loom. Thermocouple cables carry information on very high temperatures to instrumentation. These are very dependent on the wiring material used, and as a result can often be costly and troublesome to install. A typical application for a thermocouple is the measurement of exhaust gas temperature (or EGT) on a highly tuned turbocharged car, in which the measurement of the gases that are present after combustion will provide good feedback on the health and set-up of the engine, turbo, fuelling and ignition. The principle of the thermocouple is based on an effect discovered in 1822 by T. J. Seebeck who realised that when there is a change of temperature in a conductor an electromotive force, (EMF) is generated (most easily thought of as a voltage).

When two differing conductors are joined together this effect is more pronounced, and provides us with a voltage that can be measured. As this voltage is proportional to the amount of heat applied, this measurement can be used to determine just how much heat the thermocouple junction is experiencing. However, this effect could become measurably apparent in *any* junction in the thermocouple cable, and therefore care has to be taken that a minimum of joints are used, as with every joint there is an increase in the probability of inaccuracy. Another consideration is the application of interference from any other system which could be capable of generating an EMF, and therefore could, theoretically, affect the reading being given by the thermocouple (although this is equally true of any quantative measuring device). Therefore, thermocouple wiring should be chosen with great care, and with reference to any information the supplier of the thermocouple can provide.

Another type of wiring that has become something of a market leader is System 25. This was introduced to motorsport by Tony James in early 1982 on the Lotus Formula One cars campaigned under chief mechanic Bob Dance. Tony introduced a wiring loom that was standardised between the cars, allowing for easier servicing and making it simpler to change components between cars. The system that he introduced was largely based on the wiring used in aviation for many years, but as time went on, and his self-branded business became more of a full-time concern, the system began to evolve to suit the requirements of racing.

System 25 is manufactured by Raychem, and the latest evolution utilises the same connectors as used on the Eurofighter Typhoon aircraft, but modified subtly, to make them more suitable for a competition car. Connector sizes have shrunk considerably as well, meaning that for low-current devices (which are becoming more and more common on fully instrumented high-end competition cars) smaller diameter cables can be used safely, thus taking up less space and saving valuable weight.

The use of System 25 cabling has a number of advantages including high-quality gold-plated copper terminals which reduces resistance and increases reliability at cable terminations. Also, high-density plugs result in cable runs consisting of smaller cables with the associated weight and space savings and aerospace-specification cables have a good resistance to oil, fuel and heat. However, like all premium equipment, these advantages are countered by the financial cost. That said, there is very little dispute as to the quality of the system, and its popularity in top-end motorsport is a testament to this.

Resistance to fuel and oil is one of the most important qualities of a loom produced specially for motorsport. During the manufacturing process cables are surrounded by the insulation designed to protect the core from short circuits, corrosion and chafing. Despite this layer of protection, it is necessary to breach this defensive mantle whenever the cable needs to be terminated. If the termination is carried out at a point where oil or fuel is likely to collect then it is inevitable that some of the invasive fluids will seep into the space between the conductor and the insulator. This naturally present gap serves to assist capillary action, which draws the fluid further into the cable, meaning corrosion can carry on unnoticed a great distance from where the fluid actually entered the wire. As the cable is eroded by the presence of corrosive fluids (such as water) its ability to carry a current is depleted so that a cable which was previously rated to fairly high amperage may be reduced to a mere shadow of its former abilities. The results of this can be dangerous, possibly even resulting in the failure of an important component, or even a fire.

If moisture or corrosion affect the connector itself, it is possible that the change in resistance will cause the generation of heat, or in a quantity-measuring system (such as a temperature gauge) affect the reading on the gauge or value recorded on the telemetry. One possible solution to help minimise this problem is the provision of a loop of cable just before the cable enters the weatherproofing around the plug. A cable loop means that any fluids flowing along the outside of the cable will pool at the lowest point of the loop, and should not flow any further in either direction. Of course, this does mean that more space is taken up by the cable, with the weight and complexity penalties that this entails.

It is far more effective to carry out an extensive protection of the cable where the wires enter the connector, but this makes it more complicated to modify the loom at a later date. The most effective form of protecting the cable is to use heat shrink, which is a plastic coating which is slipped over the section of cable that needs to be protected. When heat is applied to the heat shrink it reduces its diameter to that of the media it is covering. This can be used to seal rubber boots that cover the back of the connectors to prevent the ingress of oil, and it also reduces the damage that can be inflicted by physical strain on the cable.

One of the biggest enemies of the wiring loom is physical damage, either from an excess of cable tension or chafing of the cable. Cables do not like to be bent at extreme angles or to be under any form of tension. The choice of cable will make a big difference to its resistance of these problems, although the best solution is to lay the cable in such a way that the damage is less likely to occur in the first place. If a cable is chosen for its resistance to damage, remember that this hardiness comes at a cost; usually it is of a greater weight, and almost certainly more expensive. Often a harder grade of insulation will result in reduced flexibility in the loom, which makes it more difficult to run the cable along bulkheads etc.

If after all your careful loom planning and neat wiring, there are still sections where the cable has no alternative but to run up against sharp edges and areas of abrasion or heat, the best method of protection is to provide a protection to the loom specifically at the point of potential damage. This protection can take the form of a spiral binding made from polythene, which is mentioned in slightly more detail in Chapter 3. Normally this material is used to protect and hold together a loom that would otherwise be unkempt and easily damaged. However, if only localised protection is required the technique for applying it is slightly different. Assuming the loom has already been completed and the extra protection is to be added, then the process is relatively straightforward. The spiral binding is wound tightly around the cable loom at the area which is liable to be damaged, and the cable is tied at each end to prevent movement. As it is quite likely that this area of loom is at an angle the wrap is unlikely to cover it comprehensively.

There are two ways that adequate protection can be achieved. The first is to wrap the loom so that the protective coating overlaps on the inside of the radius, and butts together on the outside edge. This gives the maximum protection, but it is virtually impossible to be carried out neatly. The finished article is bulky and cumbersome, and uses more spiral wrap than is necessary. If however the spiral wrap is wound so that it butts together neatly on the *inside* radius, the wrap will be spaced out on the outside radius. This should still provide protection for the cabling (despite leaving some of the original loom exposed) yet is infinitely neater and less cumbersome than the first

OVERLEAF *The more confidence you have in your components the harder you can push your machine.* (Theunis du Plessis)

technique. It should be noted that the tighter the radius of the bend, the more spaced out the spiral wrap will be on the outer side. Also note that tighter bends mean wires are under increased stress and are more prone to failure.

Even where extra protection has been provided for the loom, it is important to maintain vigilance where known areas of chafing or other cable damage are prevalent. It is good practice to examine any loom while working in that area, no matter what task is being carried out. For example, it is a question of only a few extra seconds of your time to give a quick visual inspection of cables near to where a basic fluid level check is being carried out. A quick clean with a cloth or similar may expose evidence of overheating (such as discoloration of the insulation) or cracking and chafing of the insulation, all of which could have disastrous consequences if not noticed.

System 25 has an operating temperature of up to 150°C, but it is only resistant to oils up to 70°C. Therefore, if exposure to hot oils or other fluids can be minimised then cable life is certain to be extended. If it is anticipated that extremes of temperatures are likely to be experienced (turbochargers often reach in excess of 600°C; way beyond what our cables are capable of withstanding), then silvered heat-resistant sleeving is a good way of reducing the temperatures encountered by the loom within.

The silvered surface creates an effective barrier to the thermal radiation that hot components discharge, meaning that anything that is the other side of this protective barrier will maintain a lower temperature than other unprotected components in the same harsh environment. Of course, the temperature is still likely to be higher than that encountered in places with less highly stressed mechanical components, but there are times when exposing cable looms to high temperatures cannot be avoided. As long as these precautions are taken, and the correct grade of cable has been selected, there should be no problems.

Whilst many under-bonnet components may be subjected to extremes of heat, certain other items around the vehicle (such as rain lights, telemetry potentiometers, wiper motors etc) may be subjected to rain and dirt ingress, which is just as harmful. Surprisingly to some, damage from foreign objects such as grit is often a lot more harmful than the presence of water; many an expensive telemetry potentiometer has had its life shortened by the unwanted ingress of dirt to its delicate internals. Therefore, it is an economically sound principle to try to make sure that components on the vehicle are sealed from potentially harmful intruders, or if this is not practical, at least give the opportunity for unwanted fluids to drain away.

With some components there will be little problem with sealing them entirely from the outside world; a good example is the humble rain light. However, it is more practical to seal an LED rain light than a traditional filament type. The reasoning is simple: an LED light is less prone to failure, and will therefore not really need to be opened so a silicon sealant (such as readily available bathroom sealant) can be used to seal the points at which the lens and the body of the lamp meet. A filament lamp only has a limited life, and may therefore need to be opened for replacement. As well as requiring access, a filament lamp generates a fair amount of heat, something an LED lamp is not guilty of. Therefore if any leaks develop (which is more likely bearing in mind the constant heating/cooling cycle that occurs) then air and water from the atmosphere are likely to be sucked into the cooling lamp housing after the bulb is switched off. This will rapidly attack the silvered coating of the lamp. In fact, where a lighting cluster is retaining water, often the simplest technique to minimise the damage is to drill a small hole at the lowest point of the lens where the water collects, allowing it to drain away. However, this should *not* be attempted with glass lenses or sealed-beam lights!

There are a myriad of sensors under the bonnet, some of which utilise very delicate techniques to monitor the health of the engine, or the loads and requirements that are placed upon it. It used to be common to measure the amount of air an engine was consuming by putting a flap into the airflow, which was then attached to a potentiometer that sent a signal to the ECU. From this signal the exact amount of fuel to be added to the engine for a correct stoichiometric ratio could be calculated. However, the wiper in the potentiometer of this system could be severely reduced in its accuracy by the presence of dirt or oil. By sealing the unit as effectively as possible, using silicone sealant where necessary, the reliability of these units can be improved by excluding any detritus that could have a derogatory effect on the sensor's operation.

It is not viable to go around the engine bay sealing absolutely every component you can lay your hands upon, but during component installation think about the conditions in which it will be living. Certain sealants are not resistant to heat, or are more likely to be degraded by oil and fuel. For items not likely to be subjected to excessive heat or exposed to oils, a standard bathroom-type sealant is quite suitable. These sealants are very useful, mainly because of their inherent flexibility. It is of course possible to use Araldite or similar to weatherproof items, but despite the fact that this is an excellent adhesive, it lacks flexibility. This means that if an item needs to flex, as a rubber boot on a connector may for example, such a substance would break, allowing unwanted contaminants to enter the boot.

Flexible sealants should be used with care however as when resealing an item it is tempting to simply plaster the sealant over the top of the existing disturbed seal. This procedure rarely creates a seal that is as capable as a fresh one on a clean surface. It really is a matter of taking a few moments to clean off the old sealant before applying more. Degreasing the surface is also vitally important as even the best sealants will not adhere to something if it is covered by a film of oil. Oil and grease act as lubricants by placing a thin layer on the two moving surfaces in contact with each other, thereby reducing friction. It is this property which prevents sealants and adhesives from sticking when you try to apply them to a surface that has not been degreased.

When degreasing or otherwise cleaning components, ask yourself if the component will be affected by the cleaning media you intend to use. Another consideration is that certain chemicals can be given off while sealant is curing, which can be harmful to certain sensors. The Lambda sensor is a probe placed in the flow of exhaust gases and uses either zirconium dioxide or titanium dioxide to detect unburnt oxygen in the exhaust gases of the car. This then forms a closed loop feedback to adjust the mixture (via the ECU) to try to get the fuel/air ratio as accurate as possible. Due to the specialised materials that comprise these sensors they tend to be rather prone to damage by the fumes given off by curing sealant. As these sensors are not very cheap, it is definitely a mistake you don't want to make too often!

Choosing the type of termination for your cables can be a point of heated debate in some circles. Many people do not agree with the use of crimped connectors in vehicles, and I have seen many articles in magazines of apparently good standing that denounce them wholeheartedly. (Magazines which, incidentally, include articles on fitting electrical items using Scotch-lok connectors!) The aviation industry however, crimps almost all the connectors used in aircraft. The difference between the high quality, safe and secure crimps used in aviation, and the sometimes substandard types used by the average car enthusiast, is almost always traceable to the tools used. Crimping tools used in the aviation industry cost many hundreds of pounds, and have regular checks to ensure that they are capable of producing high-quality joints. Part of an aviation engineer's training is on precision termination tools (or PTT), and the tools even come with a gauge to check that the tool has not been worn beyond set tolerances before it is used.

All this is quite a way from the crude, glorified pliers that inhabit the bottom of most engineers' tool boxes. Whilst it is not really necessary to purchase crimping tools that cost the same as the average tool chest, for a moderate outlay it is possible to buy a set of crimping pliers that will produce reliable, strong and highly conductive terminations with a minimum of effort. The best types are those that are made up of many layers of pressed steel. These produce straight joints, something which is important when crimping. A joint which is slightly twisted when crimped will not apply pressure to the conductor evenly, meaning that the joint will not be strong when placed under tension. If crimped connectors are mounted on items such as switches, it is important to remember to cover the exposed sections of the crimp with insulation to prevent short circuits. Ideally, the heat shrink discussed earlier could be used.

If a switch is designed to be removed from the panel in the event of a fault, remember to include enough wire behind the switch (or indicator lamp and so on) to allow it to be pulled from its place while still connected. It is easier to connect and disconnect a component when there is enough slack in the wiring to allow it to be unshipped first. Often, the first time you notice that a wire is too short to allow the component to come out of its snug home is the first time you try to remove it under pressure! When crimping, ensure the wire is clean and freshly stripped; the presence of any grease or dirt on the wire prior to crimping into a terminal will result in poor conduction, and will also increase the chance of the wire pulling free. Some people like to twist the strands of the wire slightly before inserting them in the crimp and I believe this is a good practice, as it holds the strands together and prevents them from escaping from the crimp. On the other hand, some people frown on this technique, claiming that it can weaken the wire where it enters the termination.

Soldering is considered to be a reliable technique, but it is not without its drawbacks. Before we discuss the advantages and disadvantages of soldering, we should consider a few points of technique. First, a soldering iron of between 15w and 30w will be fine for most tasks. Higher wattage irons do not run any hotter, but they can apply heat to larger terminals better than a lower wattage iron, so unless you anticipate soldering terminals the size of a garden spade a standard iron is sure to suffice! Some people swear by irons that have a variable temperature control, but to be honest, this is applying more complexity and size to what should be a simple and compact device. A temperature of around 300° to 350°C is normal for most soldering. However, with lead-based solder soon to be banned from sale due to increasing legislation with relation to such products, it becomes necessary to utilise its replacement. This is rather more difficult to use and requires an iron running at a slightly higher temperature to produce a neat joint.

Cleanliness is of vital importance as the solder is unlikely to 'wet', or cover the joint if it is dirty. When applying the solder, the two areas to be joined should be 'tinned' first. This is the process of applying solder to both halves of the joint to ensure there is maximum adhesion between the two when the actual joint is made, and there are no spots remaining which are not covered with solder. Once each side has been tinned, the terminal can be heated (bearing in mind that excess heat could damage the component), until the solder melts, and the tinned wire introduced. After the solder on the wire has melted, the joint can be allowed to cool and it should be complete after one or two seconds. It is a good idea to slide some heat shrink over the wire *before* the joint is soldered together, but do not forget to move it sufficiently far up the wire to prevent the heat of the iron shrinking it prematurely. This can then be moved over the soldered joint after it has cooled, and then heated mildly to induce the shrinkage. Be aware that an excess of heat at this stage can melt the solder you had applied previously, so be careful where you point your heat gun!

Well spaced switch gear helps to minimise driver error ...

The advantages of soldering are immediately obvious: it is a secure form of joining and easily provides the best conductivity of the termination methods we have discussed. On the down side, it can be difficult to do at short notice, requires the availability of a soldering iron, and means that joints cannot be connected and disconnected at a whim. It also introduces rigidity into the cores of the cable which could result in conductor fracture in high stress or high vibration situations. However, for reliability, there is little that can be better than a soldered joint and a cable is often more likely to snap than a soldered joint pull free. The trick is soldering a joint *well*. It is all too easy to create a poor joint (known as a dry joint) which has poor conductivity, and it is only with practice that consistently good results can be achieved.

One other terminal to discuss is the Scotch-lok. Its proper name is the insulation displacement connector, and it is manufactured by 3M. Whilst it may have its uses (it is convenient to use and requires no special tools) it is not in common use in motorsport. They may be ideal for creating temporary or prototype designs, but it is best to stay with more permanent methods when building looms or installing components for competition cars.

The most important part of selecting a component for a task is to ensure that it is suitable for the loads it will have placed upon it, the harsh conditions it may encounter, the space it must occupy, and that it is of as low a weight as is reasonably possible. A component which has been industrialised to make it ultra robust and strong and is only intended as a switch to operate the blower fan for example, is likely to be far too heavy, bulky and hard to operate for the task in hand. Consider the current ratings for your components; do they match the cabling you are using for the task?

If you are uprating a component, are there likely to be any disadvantages? For example, a swap from a 55w headlight bulb to a 100w bulb is likely to result in degraded reliability, and increased fragility of the filament due to its decreased diameter. On average the filament life is halved so is it really worth the effort for the extra 45w of lighting? Every upgrade must be assessed. There is no point in buying a

It is only when harsh conditions are experienced that the wiring you have built will show its weaknesses. (PIAA UK)

lightweight competition alternator to shave a little weight from the car, and then finding that it is not capable of running the monster lighting rig you are hanging from the front of your vehicle. Consider also the environment the component is to inhabit. In the case of a component which is regularly exposed to heat it may be possible to purchase one that is capable of withstanding increased temperatures, but you will obviously pay a premium for any such item that has better characteristics than a standard part.

Chapter 3

Modifying existing looms and systems

IN THE COMPETITION car builder's search for an ever lighter car, it is immediately apparent that the wiring loom fitted as standard to a production vehicle is not ideally suited to the task of racing. Designed to last the conceivable lifetime of the vehicle (or the length of the manufacturer's warranty at least), the standard loom is often over-engineered compared with the loom of, for example, a single-seater. However, there are situations in which a wiring loom is not up to the extra demands that motorsport may place upon it. This will be examined in this chapter.

Redundant systems

When sitting in the driving seat of a standard production car there are many systems, immediately visible, that are surplus to requirements. The amount of work required to dispose of these unwanted items varies, and certain factors need to be taken into account. For example, with a car that may later be returned to road specification it would be unwise to remove wiring systems only to have to refit them at a later stage. Sometimes it may be necessary to retain items that could be discarded in a different racing series to that in which you are competing. The Camel Trophy Landrover Discoveries for example, were fitted with manual winding front windows and electric windows at the rear. This allowed for easy operation of the rear windows from the front seat, while ensuring that the front windows would still operate in the event of an emergency, such as a total immersion of the vehicle during a river crossing. Obviously this is not a requirement that most competition vehicles face, but it is a good example of how a vehicle's electrical system can be tailored to suit the specific requirements of the sport in hand.

There are two extremes of electrical preparation for a car destined for competition. One is the total removal of the electrical system, leaving only that which is required to run the engine and provide a basic instrumentation to the driver. For this situation it will probably be less effort and more suited to its purpose if the loom is built entirely from scratch. Making new looms is covered fully in Chapter 4. At the other extreme is the vehicle which does not deviate too much from the manufacturer's original design, in which case the original loom can be modified appropriately.

It is a common modification to remove the side and rear windows of a competition car and replace them with polycarbonate; either due to regulations specifying this, or purely as a move to reduce weight and improve safety. Naturally, the window mechanism would be removed at the same time although a significant amount of weight is taken up by the wiring loom for these windows and is often left behind the door skin. If access is available, this wiring should be removed, but it would be better practice to go even further and extract all the cables that feed the system, right from the operating switches and motors to the fusebox. It should be noted that often a fuse feeds more than one system, so it is important to make sure that the wiring system you are removing does not feed anything else that is required to be operated.

When a cockpit ventilation system is in operation, it is common to use the blower fan fitted by the manufacturer of the vehicle. This is a good practice as the manufacturer spent a great deal of time and money ensuring that the fan was fit for the purpose, and capable of demisting the windows and providing airflow to passengers. However, certain elements of the electrical system can be dispensed with. Blower fans tend to be fitted with more than one speed. Speed control is usually achieved by the insertion of a resistance in series with the motor, which is selected by the blower switch mounted in the cockpit. This system can be simplified by the removal of the speed control; most drivers are not worried about variable speeds, although of course, this is a matter of personal preference. The entire speed control system can therefore be dispensed with and replaced by a simple on/off switch. The advantages of this set-up are immediately apparent: reduced clutter of the driver's controls, extra space on the dashboard for more important system switching, and reduced weight and complexity.

If the vehicle is to be kept road legal then it is worth checking with an MoT tester that any systems you plan to remove are not part of the annual test. A good example of this is the rear fog lamp, the fitting of which is only mandatory for vehicles manufactured after October 1979. Unless there is a specific requirement for one in your race regulations then it is a useful weight saving to dispense with it. However, on a car built after this date removing the rear fog lamp will put you in breach of the Road Vehicle Lighting Regulations 1989 if the vehicle is used on public roads.

Tidy wiring is easier to maintain and looks more professional. (Paul Martin)

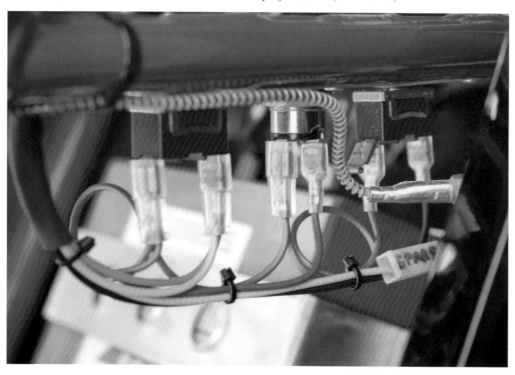

If it is necessary to retain a system to pass either the MoT test or to comply with the regulations of your desired type of motorsport, then it is sometimes possible to replace items with smaller or lighter equivalents. A horn is required by law in a motor vehicle, yet those fitted to most cars are larger than is really needed. A motorcycle horn of the correct voltage is almost certainly going to be lighter and more compact, while still fulfilling the requirements of the MoT legislation.

Competition spec starter motors are available which utilise a reduction gearing meaning the motor spins at a higher speed when cranking the engine and the output is geared down to produce more torque at a lower speed. Therefore, the starter motor unit can be smaller and thus lighter, and will often draw less current than the original. The knock-on effect of this is that a smaller battery can be carried, saving further weight. Of course, these advantages usually come at a price as such units are necessarily more expensive than their less advanced, heavier counterparts.

Utilising standard instruments

As a rule, accurate aftermarket gauges are not the cheapest components. With certain instrumentation accuracy is not of paramount importance, for example, water temperature. It is not vital to know your water is exactly 88°C, but it is pretty important to make sure that a coolant overheat is clearly shown. For this purpose the standard gauge will probably do the job adequately, especially as it is usually located in the neat instrument binnacle ideally placed in the driver's line of sight. However, an accurate rev counter is of more importance. Whilst the average supermarket shuttle-

Considerably cheaper than a data logger, this kitchen stopwatch fits quite neatly into this dashboard.

run provides few redline moments, a racing vehicle is almost permanently in the top half of its usable rpm range.

A non-standard engine will almost certainly have a much higher redline than its production counterpart, and thus a different rev counter will be required. If the vehicle's other standard instruments are being retained then it is an advantage to be able to position the competition rev counter in the same place that its domestic equivalent was situated previously. More often than not it is easier to create a bespoke dashboard, putting all the gauges of direct interest to the driver during competition, directly in his line of sight, having removed all instrumentation which is of no interest. Standard vehicle wiring looms rarely lend themselves to this modification however and a large amount of time and effort can be expended trying to decode the instrument cluster wiring so that it can be adapted to a non-standard dash. The selection and fitting of rev counters is covered in Chapter 9.

If the car that has been chosen as a base for the competition vehicle is of fairly lowly specification then it could be that some instruments are not fitted as standard. For those on a budget, the possibility of using an instrument cluster from a higher spec car in the same model range could be considered. However, this is never going to provide the same level of accuracy and user customisation as a custom-made item using instruments chosen by the car's constructor.

Another thing that should be considered is the ergonomics of the standard dashboard when used in the race environment. A brilliantly designed instrument cluster may be perfectly visible from the driver's seat in normal, everyday use, but combine a smaller steering wheel with a bucket seat in a position that is totally different to its road equivalent, and suddenly gauges that were perfectly visible before are impossible to see when the driver is strapped in.

Paring down and rebuilding a loom

When you have decided which systems are no longer required you can begin to think about removing the appropriate wiring. There are two alternatives: strip the loom out in situ, or remove it and trim it down on the bench. Whilst the first option may seem to be the easiest, the time you save by not removing the loom will be offset by the added inconvenience of having to work in and around the vehicle's structure. Removing the loom will also allow for a neater construction while giving the opportunity to inspect cables for chafing and damage.

Modifying the loom on the bench

If the loom is constructed in sections this task is made infinitely easier, as it is possible to remove just those you intend to deal with. Cables are normally wrapped with a self adhesive tape, which will need to be removed to gain access to the loom. This can be reused, but will not look very nice, or provide the same amount of protection as using brand new tape. Perhaps the neatest option is spiral wrap, made from polythene. Used extensively in the aviation industry, it provides an anti-chafe covering for cables, allows for easy modification of looms, and can be reused when modifications are made. However, it is important to apply this tape properly, otherwise it provides very little protection at all.

When you have decided how much loom you will need to remove it is necessary to disconnect it from the items it is attached to electrically. First, the car should be electrically isolated, disconnecting the battery and any other sources of electrical power. Every single connection that is disconnected should be marked clearly. The simplest way of doing this is with masking tape, which is wrapped around the connector, and written on with a permanent marker. If the loom is likely to be

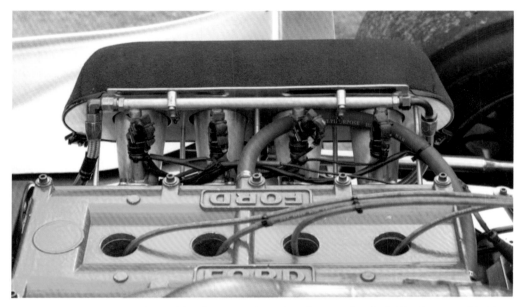

Despite having relatively few cables the wiring has already started to look like the proverbial 'rats nest'! Note also the potential for chafing where the HT leads leave the camshaft cover. (Paul Martin)

removed for some time then bear in mind that masking tape is not designed to remain adhered over a long period, and its glue changes properties in time. It either dries up, causing the label to drop off, or turns to a sticky mess, creating a nasty residue to be left on the cable. A relatively simple job can look a lot more intimidating when all your carefully prepared labels are staring at you from the floor of the workshop as you hold the loom in your hands!

If you mark every cable as it is removed with as much information as you feel is needed, then the job of refitting can be greatly simplified. As you unwind (or cut off) the old looming material you will find that cables leave the loom, usually at 90°. At each one a tie-wrap should be placed either side of the cable exit point, so that the position at which the cables rejoin the loom can be maintained. If tie-wraps are placed evenly along the length of the loom as the covering is removed then it is easier to maintain the shape of the loom on the bench. When the cables have been entirely stripped of their protective wrap they can be inspected for damage and chafing. If evidence of chafing is apparent, then good practice dictates that the cable should be replaced with one of identical current rating, unless of course, it is due to be removed as part of the loom reduction. An in-line repair could be carried out, but the only time these are really acceptable is as a 'get-you-home', and as the cable is laid bare on the bench there really is no excuse for such short cuts!

In the event of a single cable needing replacement, the new one should be led along the path of the old cable, following its path and curves. The old cable should be pulled through the tie-wraps (or if needed, the tie-wrap can be removed) one by one, and the new cable tie-wrapped alongside the loom. As all the wraps will be removed as the new cable coating is installed, neatness of their installation is not a priority. The process of cable replacement should follow from one end of the loom to the other, with the new cable being fitted as the old one is removed. When the process is complete the loom should appear exactly as it did before the new cable was fitted, but without the damage.

It is important to find out why the chafing took place so an inspection of the point at which the damage occurred needs to be carried out. This section of the loom should then be marked for extra protection, however it must be remembered that adding extra sheathing to the loom at this stage may make it less flexible which could cause some problems when refitting it. The part of the car that caused the damage should also be inspected and any sharp corners of metal smoothed if at all possible. If the problem cannot be overcome in this way then rerouting of the loom should be carried out. Sometimes, moving a loom a matter of millimetres can be enough to rectify a persistent problem.

Now is the time to add any extra systems if required. New cables should be added to the loom using a similar method to that employed when replacing damaged ones, ensuring that the cable used is of a sufficiently high rating to carry the current loads required. It is helpful to provide a fair bit of extra cable at either end to ensure that some versatility is allowed for when locating new items. The excess cable can be trimmed off when the new system is firmly fixed in place and a permanent termination has been carried out. It is easier to trim off excess than find extra cable when it is discovered that it is too short!

Another type of damage which may become apparent at this time is burning or melting of the cable insulation. Burning can either be because of an overload of the cable, or from an external heat source such as an exhaust manifold. The cable could have been overloaded due to current being demanded that it was never designed to carry. Slaving driving lamps directly into the main-beam circuit without a relay is a classic example of this. The cable could have been replaced with another which was not rated high enough to carry the current required, as a result of a badly repaired loom for example. Alternatively, the component supplied by the cable may have failed, causing excessive current to be drawn.

If the source of heat damage is external then there are a number of alternative ways of preventing this from reoccurring. The best technique is to move the loom away from where the heat is produced. Obviously this is not always possible, so some form of external protection should be applied instead. Such protection is provided by an aluminised heat-reflective wrap or sleeve, which is applied around the cables in the form of a tape (usually with an adhesive backing), or a shroud through which the cable is passed. As the shroud is basically an open-ended tube, one end of the wiring to be protected needs to be disconnected to allow the sleeve to be fitted. Again, this is a job which is much easier on the bench.

In a case of heat damage caused by an overloading of the cable, it is vital to find out the cause. If the component has failed, the fuse should burn out, protecting the cabling from damage, but if the fuse has failed to 'pop', then further investigation needs to be carried out. Was the fuse suitably rated for the component it was supplying? Where a system is supplied with a circuit breaker, was the CB operating correctly? This can be checked by carefully, and briefly, shorting the live output from the circuit breaker to earth. If it does not 'pop' to an open state then it is faulty. However, it should be mentioned that circuit breakers very rarely fail in the 'closed' position, preferring to open themselves if an internal fault develops.

With the loom completed it is important to replace its protective covering before it is refitted. To make a neat job using the hard, polythene spiral wrap there are certain procedures that should be followed. First, it is important to ensure that the loom is wrapped while it is laid out in the way it will be mounted in the vehicle. When a loom has a 90° bend in the car then this should be replicated on the bench as the wrap is applied. If this is not carried out, difficulties may be encountered when refitting it. Secondly, it is important that the wrap is applied tightly because if it is applied loosely then it may vibrate or rub in use, causing damage to the very cable it is intended to protect. This is facilitated by starting at one end of the loom, wrapping it a few times, and adjusting the coils of spiral wrap for tightness before applying electrical tape over the loose end. On top of this electrical tape a tie-wrap should be applied, guaranteeing that the end of the spiral wrap is held firmly in place during the wrapping of the loom.

Thirdly, it is good practice to cover the smaller spurs of the loom first, leaving the trunk (or main bulk) of the loom until last. This allows the smaller sections to be incorporated into the trunk neatly. Finally, the tie-wraps that were used in the construction of the loom should be removed one by one as the spiral wrap is wound up to the point on the loom where they are situated. They should be left in place as long as possible to preserve the shape of the loom and it is now that the importance of the tie-wraps at the loom spurs becomes apparent. Whenever the end of a piece of spiral wrap is reached, it should be secured in the same manner as the start. Running a hand firmly around the loom in the direction of the spiral wrap rotation removes some of the slack and once this has been carried out the loose end can be taped and tie-wrapped down. If at a later date you decide to incorporate a new cable it is a simple matter to unclip the end nearest the point at which the cable will be added. The cable can be incorporated into the loom using the technique used previously, and the spiral wrap reapplied.

Good housekeeping means damage can be spotted before it causes a retirement, or worse ... (Elliott Russell)

Once the loom is fully protected (including heat proofing) it is ready to be reinstalled in the vehicle. Starting at one end of the loom, usually at the front of the car, the first connections are made. Common sense dictates that the loom should be connected up as we go along, thereby minimising the risk of overlooking any components to be connected. It is possible that slight adjustments of the spiral wrap need to be carried out, but this will only really become apparent as the cable is laid in place. Extra mounting of the loom can be facilitated with the use of small, self-adhesive tie-wrap mounting blocks. If these are to be used it is vital that the area they are being mounted to is clean and free from oil and grease. It is very unlikely the block will hold in place if the block is saturated with oil as the adhesive is affected badly.

Wherever possible, the loom should be fixed in such a way that movement is minimised; this reduces chafing and makes the installation much neater. Bends in the wiring loom should be kept to as large a radius as possible because tight bends have a detrimental effect on the insulation and conductivity of the cable. In the long term this could lead to reliability problems, open circuits and the failure of systems. With the loom fully in place and all systems connected, a final check should be carried out to ensure that no cables are still disconnected or shorted to earth, and then the power can be reconnected. Before any systems are switched on an in-depth check of the loom should then be carried out to ensure there has been no overheating or burning. At this point it is prudent to check every system on the car, and specifically any item

Access to the deepest recesses of your vehicle is not always as convenient as this! (Elliott Russell)

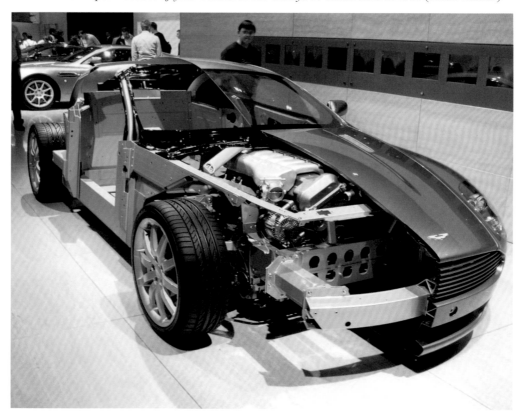

added in the loom rebuild. During each individual check the loom should be examined, and in the event of any evidence of overloading being discovered the battery must be disconnected immediately and the fault traced.

Modifying the loom in situ
Working on a loom in the car is slightly more difficult. Some sections will need to be pulled away from the car itself to allow access to the loom covering during removal, and to allow new spiral wrap to be fitted. However, the major advantage that this technique has is that very little has to be disconnected to achieve results. This means there is less chance of a mistake being made, and less testing needs to be carried out as fewer systems have been disturbed. It is important that the loom is inspected as you remove the old cable, as keeping it fitted reduces our ability to see the side of the loom nearest the bodywork. It is therefore a good idea to use a small mirror to look at the sections that would otherwise be out of sight. An old compact make-up mirror is ideal as it folds up into its own container which is robust enough to put in the tool box.

The easiest and safest way of removing the covering of the loom without damaging the cables within it is with a pair of side cutters. By sliding one of the jaws inside the open end of the loom wrap between the cables and the wrap, it is possible to carefully cut up the length of the loom, peeling back the coating as you progress. Care should be taken, as damage to any of the cables will mean that they would have to be replaced. The procedure for this is pretty much identical to that carried out with the loom on the bench.

The method of keeping the bundle of cables in place with some well placed tie-wraps is still applicable, and keeps things neat and tidy if the loom is exposed for any length of time. If any connectors are disconnected but not removed (for example electric window wiring on a car that may later return to road use) then some form of long term protection is prudent. The connector should be checked for signs of corrosion, and if this is found it should be removed. There are various products on the market that will do this, but check the information provided on the tin to confirm suitability before use.

Some types of corrosion may be hazardous, and it is sensible to take appropriate precautions before dealing with it. For example, aluminium oxide dust can be hazardous when inhaled, and therefore a dust-mask or similar should be used. Always assess the substance in hand and take safety precautions to suit. Once the corrosion has been removed and the connector is clean it is best to seal it inside a poly bag, such as a strong sandwich bag to protect it from water and dirt. The bag should be sealed using a tie-wrap, and then tie-wrapped to the loom to prevent it moving. The priority is keeping things tidy; a tidy loom is an easy-to-maintain loom. If a connector is allowed to flail around in free space it can be damaged by contact with other objects in the vehicle, or may wear the insulation from the cables that lead to it. And nothing makes your heart sink quite like the sound of something fairly important crunching beneath your feet as you slide yourself into your bucket seat...

Once the loom is ready to be recovered the technique is the same as that for a loom on the bench, but obviously hampered by it still being fitted in a confined space.

Circuit breakers

Circuit breakers (CBs)are useful in competition cars due to them being easily reset. Sadly, manufacturers tend to fit fuses in places that are not convenient for the installation of a circuit breaker. In the event of a fuse blowing, it has to be replaced, whereas a circuit breaker can be reset. This means that important circuit breakers should be placed within easy reach of the driver or co-driver. If a standard loom is being modified this is not always an easy proposition, and it is often better to rebuild the loom without the original wiring. Naturally, of course, not every system on the car requires a circuit breaker (and in some cases blade fuses can be replaced with circuit breakers that fit in the place of the fuse), and only circuits which the driver views as needing a breaker need replacing.

Of course, fuses are not without their advantages. Cheap to fit initially, the average fuse would have to blow 50 times before an aircraft-specification circuit breaker would be a viable replacement economically. Also, the light weight and simple construction of a basic fuse has to be considered. In the case of a standard loom being modified to suit competition use, circuit breakers tend to cause more problems than they solve. However, in a bespoke loom they are vital, and therefore if a hybrid loom is being created (consisting partially of a standard manufacturer's loom and partially a loom created for the purpose) it is possible to incorporate CBs into the additional parts of the system. Fuses and circuit breakers are covered more thoroughly in Chapter 5.

Moving the battery

It is usual practice to move the car's main battery from under the bonnet to the passenger cell or boot, according to what is allowed in the regulations. Whilst the mechanics of this operation are covered more fully in Chapter 6, there are considerations to be taken into account when using a vehicle's existing loom. Most cars have a large cable capable of carrying heavy current loads from the battery to the solenoid, and from the solenoid to the starter motor. On more modern units the starter motor and solenoid are often combined. From the battery post a cable is usually fed to the fusebox, where the circuit protection is carried out.

When a battery is relocated, both of these cables will need replacing with longer ones, although in the case of separate solenoid systems the smaller cable running to the fusebox can be taken from the permanently live section of the solenoid. However, the inclusion of an FIA-spec isolation switch is normally required by regulations (although even if it is not it is a prudent move to use one). It is vital that an FIA switch is fitted correctly; if improperly wired then the engine will not stop when the switch is turned off. This is due to the current supplied by the alternator being sufficient to run the engine and auxiliaries without requiring any input from the battery. The extra connections provided on the FIA spec master switch allow you to connect the ignition circuit through the cut-out, meaning that when activated the switch will not only isolate the car electrically but shut down the engine as well. The FIA switch is connected to the earth cable between the battery and the vehicle bodywork. The earth cable is normally colour coded yellow to allow quick identification. Most safety systems (such as fire extinguishers) should have a back-up or separate power supply to the normal 12-volt system. For example, electrically operated fire extinguishers use a separate battery pack to ensure that they will still operate even if the electrical system of the vehicle has failed.

Chapter 4

Building a loom from scratch

IN MANY WAYS it is easier to build a loom entirely yourself than it is to modify the original manufacturer's loom to your requirements. On a normal saloon car, the loom is manufactured to provide ease of fitting combined with minimum production costs. Of course, a single seater does not have a standard production variant, therefore the loom will have to be made specially anyway. This allows us a great deal of flexibility, and gives the builder of the car an in-depth knowledge of the vehicle that a mere modifier may never possess. There are different techniques that can be employed – either manufacturing the loom in-situ, or removing the old loom to use as a reference while you build the new one on the bench.

Building a loom entirely to your own specifications allows you to have total control of the materials used, from the insulation to the conductors, not forgetting the loom protection itself. You can follow the most convenient route through the car, as the loom no longer has to be hidden behind trim or serve hundreds of electrical devices which are not required on a racing machine. Keeping the loom to a reasonable length is one of the most important considerations. If it is too long it will be heavier than is needed, and will also provide more resistance to the path of the current.

Before we consider the design of the loom in its entirety, let us think about the process of designing a loom in modules. Whilst it is good practice to minimise the amount of breaks in a wiring system, a connector to separate the engine loom from the main vehicle loom is definitely a good investment. If you have a spare engine, this can be built with an identical loom to that on the engine that is installed in the car, and then should the power plant need to be replaced the entire unit can be electrically disconnected by the removal of one or two plugs. When the new engine is lowered into place, the new loom can be connected in the same way, saving a great deal of time. Importantly, this also reduces the risk of leaving a component disconnected, as a loom fitted on the bench allows the engine to be inspected from all angles to ensure nothing has been left unattached. It can also be attached more securely (as it will not need to be removed in a hurry) and can be better protected from the heat and oil usually present in the engine bay.

Due to the harsh environment to which the loom will be subjected, the connector should be of a high quality and capable of resisting contaminant ingress. Once assembled, the connector should be over sealed with a silicone sealant that will assist in repelling contaminating oil from the terminals. Any place that oil may be displaced, such as around oil catch cans, dipstick holes and so on should be avoided when considering a place to site the connector; the higher on the bulkhead it is placed the less likely it is to be contaminated. Make sure there is easy access to allow it to be checked for good contact in the event of an engine problem, and that nothing

prevents connectors from being connected or removed once the engine is in place. Fitting an engine and then finding that the space that should be occupied by the connector is in fact taken up by the rocker cover is disheartening to say the least!

When selecting a connector it is prudent to choose a slightly larger one than is required to include some blank pins in case more instrumentation or ECU wiring is required at a later date. If this does become the case it is a matter of minutes rather than hours to add extra wiring to the loom, allowing you to effectively 'future-proof' your competition car. A bulkhead connector also provides a good place to make the change from wiring suitable for the under-bonnet environment to cheaper, lighter and more flexible cables better suited to looming located behind the dashboard and around the cockpit.

It is possible to split the vehicle wiring loom into further smaller chunks, however, consider that every point at which a connector is placed is a possible point of unreliability. This is balanced by ease of maintenance and it is much easier to replace three feet of loom than the entire length from bulkhead to tail-lamps. In aviation, any cable damage usually results in that cable being totally replaced; an in-line repair is asking for problems. Consider this when you construct your loom: do you really need to run the loom under the driver's seat? Will the route you have chosen for the loom result in damage from driver/co-driver/equipment ingress/egress? Will any equipment have to be taken out to gain access to, or for removal of the loom?

If you can route the loom in such a way that damage is minimised then you are saving yourself a lot of effort in the long run. The loom should be supported as much as is reasonably possible. A P-clip placed at approximately every 100mm should be sufficient, but this varies, depending on the thickness of the loom and the loads likely to be placed upon it. Covering the loom with polythene spiral wrap will protect it, yet allow other cables to be easily added later, and for minor repairs to be carried out.

When putting bends in the loom remember that tight radii can result in damage to the conductors or splitting of the insulation and so needs to be avoided where possible. Anywhere that a sharp bend is unavoidable should be inspected on a regular basis to see if any visible damage has occurred. Of course, a visual inspection will not enlighten you as to the condition of the conductor beneath. Where a cable passes over a point that could cause abrasion, such as the edge of a panel or a metal lip, then extra protection needs to be applied. The first step to minimise damage to the loom is to reduce the risk from the sharp edge. This can take the form of a plastic material that is placed over the hazard, or possibly a P-clip placed in such a way that the loom is moved clear of the protrusion. When the loom has been moved to the point where no contact is possible (try moving it with your hands, and don't forget the g-forces it could come under during braking, accelerating and cornering), then no further action needs to be taken. If the loom can still make contact with the protrusion (albeit at decreased risk due to the provision of the low-friction covering) then there is still a requirement for extra protection on the loom itself. The best method is to use the spiral wrap mentioned previously to create a sacrificial covering that can be changed when worn. Such a covering, as the name suggests, is anything you place over the loom to prevent it from being damaged, but will itself become damaged in due course. It is important to keep this closely monitored and replaced when necessary.

OPPOSITE *Running a loom in a car with a space frame is easy, as the loom can be cable-tied directly to the framework.* (Elliott Russell)

OVERLEAF *Sometimes the requirements for waterproofing the electrical system are higher than you might have first imagined!* (PIAA UK)

Should the sacrificial covering become worn through to the original loom the protection will be lost, and the potential for faults to occur (or worse) will be very high. It is clear from this that if a permanent fix is to be carried out, the only sensible solution is to move the loom away from the point of abrasion using P-clips. These clips are a secure way of mounting a loom, and to place an extra clip on the loom will have a minimal weight penalty and prevent the need to constantly assess the wiring system. During construction it will save a lot of time and effort if you make the loom 'right first time'. Think about how the loom is going to be placed, and consider just how easy that loom will be to access once the car is in full race trim.

When thinking about how the wiring loom will be constructed, it helps to borrow a little from the aviation industry. Aircraft wiring systems consist of 'bus-bars', pronounced *buzz* or *bus* depending on who you talk to, and normally shortened to *bus*. Bus-bars are points on the loom that the rest of the loom stems from. For example, an aircraft might have an 'essential dc bus', literally a dc supply which feeds power to all the critical components on the aircraft. Another bus-bar might be called 'Aux dc bus', which feeds less important systems. In the case of an emergency occurring, a system known as 'load-shedding' will disconnect the *aux bus* from the power supply, while leaving the *essential dc bus* connected. This means that anything that is not critical to flight has its power supply removed, leaving more power to operate the items that are flight critical. This would be particularly important in the case of a generator failure; if all the power is lost then the aircraft will be relying on the battery to produce its dc supply (and possibly its ac supply if an emergency

A high standard of preparation means this hill-climber is easier to maintain and less likely to suffer reliability problems. (Paul Martin)

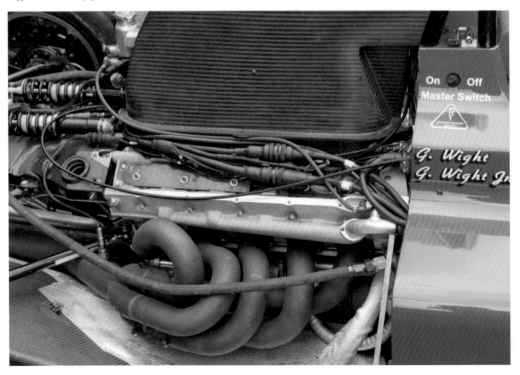

Extending vital switchgear to enable the driver to reach it is an often forgotten part of cockpit ergonomics. The car in question is a Ferrari 355. (Wren Classics)

inverter is used). If you have a limited supply of electrical power available the last thing you need is to be wasting it supplying items that are not essential to the safe flight of the aircraft.

The same could apply in competition cars, primarily those designed for endurance racing (which at circuits such as Circuit de la Sarthe could mean a very long limp back to the pit lane in the event of an electrical fault). Whilst other competition vehicles could benefit from this system, it is doubtful that others, a single seater for instance, would contain much in the way of superfluous electrical systems anyway. A rally car however is likely to contain many items that the driver could 'do without' in the case of an emergency. Auxiliary lighting, in-car communications, ventilation blower fans and certain instrumentation systems could all realistically be dropped in favour of conserving enough battery power to complete the stage in the case of a generator failure.

This automatic load shedding could occur when the ignition light comes on for a period of time greater than that which could occur due to water splash or other brief interruption of generator power. For example, if the ignition lamp should come on for greater than ten seconds a latched relay could disconnect, removing all non-essential systems from the picture. A simple push button could re-latch the relay, meaning that if the loads were accidentally removed they could easily be reinstated. This button could also be used directly after the car is started, as when using this technique the aux systems would not operate until the relay is latched closed. In some ways this is an advantage, as preventing other systems from dragging the battery voltage down during engine start will give you a greater chance of starting the vehicle, especially if the battery voltage is not very high to start with. Some people would view this method as an over complication however, and it is really up to you to decide if this is a technique that you wish to employ. Be aware however that no matter how reliable your alternator, the weak link will always be the way in which you drive it; how much do you trust your drive belt?

When setting out a loom it is important to remember to include some form of circuit protection. In some auto-cross and grass track circles it is common practice to dispense with fuses and circuit breakers altogether in the belief that it is better for the wiring to 'get a little warm' than to retire from the race due to a blown fuse. This is not an analogy I believe in; it is far better to retire with a blown fuse than to have to bail out of a rapidly incinerating valuable car!

Even if you decide not to employ the load-shedding technique detailed above it is worth thinking of grouping certain circuits together when setting up the circuit breakers. If your rain light should give reason to trip its circuit breaker then it would be pretty disastrous if that circuit breaker was also responsible for the fuel pump. However, putting the fuel pump and ignition on the same breaker, although not ideal, is less likely to prove a problem as the failure of either of these items will result in the engine stopping. Circuit breakers provide a useful means of isolating systems during fault finding, or during a race if that system proves to be faulty. It is a constant trade-off, deciding just how many CBs will be required; the more you have the greater the weight penalty, but the greater the individuality of protection.

If there is a CB for each circuit then the failure of one circuit will have the minimum of repercussions for other circuits. The downside is the sheer complexity of having hundreds of circuit breakers for every little system. On production cars it is common to have one fuse for the left-hand lights, and another for the right. This means that should one lighting system develop a fault there is still another unaffected system, thus some safety is retained. If running a system of dual redundancy (ie two fuel pumps

Neat wiring means damage is easy to spot. The wiring here is likely to be reliable due to its simplicity and sensible anti-chafe protection. The car is a 1963 Lotus 23b. (Wren Classics)

operating one at a time with the unused pump utilised in the event of the other pump failing) it would be very foolish to supply both systems from the same CB.

Hopefully, we are seeing that some systems can be grouped together, while others definitely require a circuit breaker all of their own. Bearing in mind that certain CBs could be reset mid-race it is important to place the circuit breaker panel within easy reach of the driver. As circuit breakers usually have a tell-tale white section that becomes visible when tripped, the driver could very rapidly assess which breaker has operated and reset it with the minimum interruption to his race. Of course, single-seaters are not awash with space in which to place these panels, but luckily for the teams operating such cars their electrical systems are basic to say the least.

Rally teams are likely to have a multitude of CBs dotted around the cockpit, but normally they are fortunate enough to have a co-driver who can assist with their monitoring. The advantages that come from incorporating CBs into the loom are very easy to see, but there are disadvantages as well. If operated at near their trip point, circuit breakers will often delay tripping for some time. Normally this is not possible, but it does mean that choosing the value of the CB for the circuit it is protecting needs to be carried out with care. Too high a value could result in the breaker not tripping in time to save the loom from a destructive overheat. Occasionally, CBs may trip spontaneously with neither reason nor warning. This is a rare occurrence, but it does happen all the same. It can often occur during the switching on of the system it is protecting as items such as motors and filament lamps draw a much higher current on the initial start up than during sustained operation. Circuit breakers are also a great

Don't assume that an older car will be less complex than a modern one! (Paul Parker)

deal more expensive than simple fuses, and fitting out an entire loom with CBs can become a very costly process indeed.

Before we can even think of constructing our loom we have to consider just how much material will be needed. To do this an accurate idea of how the loom will run inside the vehicle has to be determined. If we wanted lightness and considered no other options then the wires would run directly between components, practically taut between the units they are linking. Of course, this is not even slightly practical. The best technique is to draw a diagram of the vehicle viewed from above, including any electrical items that are immovable, such as the starter motor and tail lights, but leave out any item that has yet to be fitted, or could conceivably be moved. Make a couple of photocopies of this blank view if you can, the first one you draw up is unlikely to be the final copy! Now we can pencil in the wiring to the units that are immovable, remembering to include earths. Don't worry too much about individual wires; the important thing is the routing of the loom. Remember that the loom has to run a sensible route, along sills and the basic perimeter of the vehicle tends to make life easiest, and prevent the loom from being damaged.

When thinking of places to put components, consider grouping similar kinds together, or at least the ones that require similar feeds. For example, both the ECU and the shift-light need to know the engine speed, and in most cases the ECU will provide the output to the tachometer. This means that by placing the shift light control unit close to the ECU the connection can be carried out at the main ECU connector plug.

If the loom is bound tightly rather than left exposed, the risk of cable damage can be reduced. Don't forget to include some rubber in your component bracketry to isolate components from vibration. (Paul Martin)

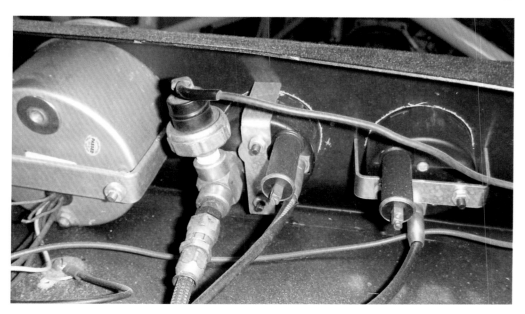

By mounting the oil pressure switch on the back of the oil pressure gauge, as seen here on an Elva racing car, the wiring can be kept as short as possible. (Wren Classics)

Conversely, putting the shift light controller directly behind the tachometer means that surplus wiring is minimised as one wire links both items. A wonderfully simple yet reliable piece of design is to place the oil pressure warning lamp switch on a T-piece, directly connected to the back of the oil pressure gauge (assuming it is a mechanical gauge of course). This means the wiring is minimised and kept within the friendlier confines of the passenger compartment. With a little thought many small savings in weight and complexity can be made, which all add up to a lighter and more reliable racing car.

Placing components low in the vehicle results in a lower centre of gravity, and thus should be encouraged wherever possible. There are some places that you should think very carefully about before siting any components there. Anything that produces an arc (such as an electric motor, relay or horn) should be placed some distance from the fuel tank, or more specifically the fuel tank vents. While the risk of explosion is small, it still does not do any harm to minimise the threat to your vehicle. Batteries vent hydrogen and oxygen when charging (even the sealed type could burst, spewing not just gas but highly corrosive electrolyte too), so it makes sense to keep these in a place where sources of ignition are unlikely. Bearing in mind that a battery that has split or leaked in some way will produce a mixture guaranteed to damage paintwork, fabric, harnesses and wiring, ensure that you place it somewhere that minimises the potential for harm if this occurs. When you are content that you have sited all of the components in places you are happy with, start drawing in the loom route. This is much easier if the car is in front of you. Use a length of fairly thick cord to simulate the cable run and you will find places that could be problematic.

Examples of difficulties you may encounter include tight radii in corners (which could cause damage to the conductors within the cable) and fouling of moving parts, both of which should definitely be avoided. This is what the planning stage is about; it is more cost effective to carry out a practice run using rope or similar than think you are going to get it right first time with expensive cables and then be proven wrong. When you have finished with your rope model it can be straightened out and measured to allow you to work out how much cable will be used. In an ideal world we would all have reels of various-sized cable suitable for every wiring situation. However, in the more modest workshops usually available to the smaller teams, you are less likely to have this luxury.

So now we have discussed modular looming, bulkhead connectors, P-clipping, bus-bars and load shedding, planning the loom routing and finally circuit breakers. Now it is time to progress to the real meat of the matter: constructing the loom itself. If the loom is constructed of modules then the best practice will be to construct one module at a time, creating a wiring diagram as you go. Don't forget that you might not be the only person working on the vehicle, so a wiring diagram will not just help you, but the next owner of the car. It makes life a lot simpler if you produce a detailed wiring diagram as you construct the loom. Include on the diagram the identification of the pins on the connectors, especially where these are likely to be complicated, such as on the bulkhead. Don't forget that the connections will be mirrored depending on which side of the plug you look; it's an easy mistake to make!

If using cable with a coloured insulation then it is easier to document exactly which cable goes where, but if single-colour cable is used then it is important that all wiring is clearly marked. Pick the item furthest from the bulkhead connector to wire up first; the following procedure applying to both the engine bay and the cockpit. Starting at this component visualise the route the cable will run. In the case of a saloon car, the furthest item towards the rear might be the tail lights. Normally, the largest cable in the

A professionally made loom, complete with anti-abrasive sheathing.

loom is the earth wire, so this is the cable I would lay first. Choose an earthing point that will guarantee a good conductivity with the bodywork of the car, removing all paint from under the terminal. The best termination for an earthing point is a ring terminal directly bolted to the vehicle chassis. You may decide to dispense with an earthed chassis entirely, relying on an earth cable linking the component, or you might consider this is a good idea if using glass-fibre bodywork. My recommendation is to use the chassis as your earth return to minimise weight and complexity, even if the panels are non-metallic.

Once you have mounted your terminal to the earth point, run it back to the component to be earthed and being the first cable in your loom, it will to an extent, dictate the initial routing. Do not terminate the connector yet; that is the last stage after the entire loom has been laid in place. Allow for some excess wiring so you can move the route that the cable follows, should this become necessary. You can hold this proto-loom in place temporarily with very loose cable ties mounted in self-adhesive blocks. Mount these in approximately the places you wish the cable to run, bearing in mind that you will need a suitable place to fit the P-clips. When this first cable has been laid in place the second cable can be fitted. All the cables from this point can be roughly taped in place at the component's connector, and then traced from the component to their destination.

In the case of tail lights, the work carried out so far would consist of an earth lead going from the tail lamp housing to the earthing terminal on the bodywork, and a lead from the tail light filament terminal, running the length of the vehicle to the lighting switch. As there is likely to be more than one light that requires a feed from this switch,

When cockpit complexity is high, clear marking of the switches is a necessity. (Elliott Russell)

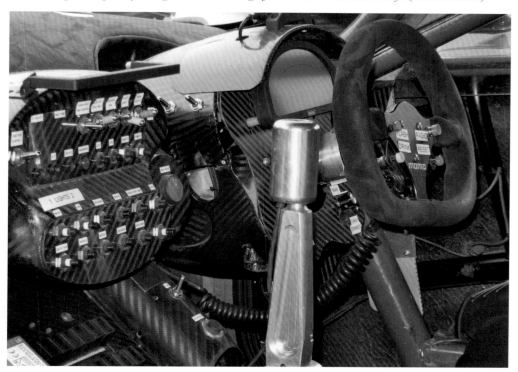

a suitable point needs to be selected to feed the other lamps at the rear, as it would be foolish to have a separate cable for each tail and numberplate lamp. As these lamps would probably be in parallel it would be quite feasible to take a second wire from the tail lamp terminal for the next component (which will have a separate earth lead). Be sure to connect these components in parallel, as in series they would barely glow!

An alternative method is to have a junction from which all the lighting feeds are taken at the rear of the car. This means a heavy duty cable capable of supplying all the current for the tail lights would run the length of the car, terminating at a terminal block from which smaller diameter cables would separate off to supply each lighting component individually. This would be neater, more reliable and easier to maintain. So now we have the earth lead in place, and the feed to operate the lamps, the other lighting feeds (indicators and such) can be placed into the loom using the same technique. When the components at the far end of the vehicle have been wired, the next furthest component from the bulkhead can be wired in. The technique is the same, and once this is complete the loom *between* the two furthest components can be covered with spiral polythene wrap, or cable tied to hold it together. This process is repeated until the loom is complete, right up to the bulkhead connector, which provides a good opportunity to go through the loom and check that nothing has been missed out. When you are happy with the loom, terminate each of the component's loom branches with the connector of your choice (cutting the excess cable down to the correct length as you go), finishing by wrapping all of the branches with spiral wrap or wiring loom tape.

By keeping the wiring neat and firmly cable-tied, the reliability and ease of servicing are substantially improved. (Paul Martin)

If you are not feeling confident about your loom (although assuming you have taken your time and been methodical there should be no problems!) you can connect it up and test the various components, checking all the time for any evidence of short circuits or wiring faults, such as overheating of cables. It would be prudent to have a carbon dioxide fire extinguisher to hand at this point. If the loom is only complete up to the bulkhead connector but no further, the other loom will have to be finished before the whole system can be checked. As soon as you are totally happy with the loom, the P-clipping can be started.

This can be quite tedious, but you have to be alert while carrying out this task. Move the loom as far away from the area of the bodywork as you can when drilling as it would heartbreaking to damage the loom with your drill after doing this much work. Remember to keep tight bends to a minimum, and avoid running the loom over sharp protrusions as much as is physically possible.

Any unsupported lengths of loom or even individual cables hanging free should be avoided as much as possible. Wherever these exist they need to be secured to the surrounding bodywork, looms or pipelines using cable ties. Cable can become damaged while on the reel, so it is best for it to be checked as it is positioned by running it through your fingers, feeling for any damage to the insulation. Once the damaged section of cable has been cut from the main length you can use the resulting shorter piece elsewhere in the vehicle.

Comprehensive dashboard systems are now available that incorporate a whole range of display configurations to keep the driver informed of the health of his vehicle. Most of these systems come with a comprehensive wiring loom that is incorporated in the vehicle as needed. Some of those on the market come complete with all the senders required as a total package, and are well worth considering for the competitor on a budget. As well as being convenient such dashboard layouts reduce the complexity of the dash and associated wiring, reducing the workload of the poor sap having to build the thing. There are systems which are capable of displaying vehicle speed and odometer readings, making them ideal for a competition vehicle that has to be road legal.

Chapter 5

Duplexing, redundancy and fail-safes

OUR MAIN CONSIDERATION when creating a loom, which is more important even than weight saving, is that of reliability. It is a well touted cliché in racing circles that 'to finish first, first you have to finish', and as this old adage has more than a shred of truth in it, it is worth bearing this in mind when we build our competition car. Racing is an environment that puts components of every kind under very high stress and is the reason why motorsport is so useful to car manufacturers to assist in the development of their more domesticated vehicles.

Motor racing provides the very extremes of every situation that a road car could experience. For example, the under-bonnet temperatures experienced by a competition car may be double that of a road car, the accelerative and declarative forces encountered will be much greater than a road car could be capable of due to the increased traction and power available. Keeping systems reliable can be achieved in a number of ways. Using cables that are rated slightly higher than is required will reduce the chance of overheating if a higher current draw is experienced. If it is close to the rating of the circuit breaker it may not be sufficient to trip it. Of course, the penalty here will be weight and flexibility of the loom. Using high quality connectors for every part of the loom means that there is less likely to be a problem due to intermittent connections, dirt or water ingress etc.

When an engineer designs a racing chassis it is a common design principle to incorporate weak points in the suspension, designed to shear just before the suspension unit is torn from the car. This means that in the event of an accident severe enough to cause the vehicle to lose its suspension components the body shell is prevented from coming to too much harm. It does seem strange to think that someone would intentionally weaken such an important structure, but plenty of strength is retained for normal in-race use, and the weak point will only come into play should an impact severe enough to disable the car occur. You may be wondering what relevance this has to our electrical systems; the point is that we include deliberate weak links in our systems, even though this could disable the vehicle in some circumstances.

A fuse (short for fusible link) is a link of wire designed to melt when too much current is drawn through it. This means that in a situation where a malfunction has occurred (such as a chafe in the wire, burnt out motor etc) the fuse will blow, interrupting the circuit and preventing further damage. There are a few basic types of automotive fuse in current use, the most common (and in my opinion the best designed) system is the blade fuse. Consisting of a plastic cartridge which slots into place on the fuse box, the blade fuse is colour coded to allow the user to quickly and easily identify the rating. The terminals it uses are coincidentally the same size as spade connectors; something that proves useful if you need to fit one into a circuit away from the main fuse box. Due to its construction it is possible to check if a blade fuse has blown by looking into the window in its side, which allows the user to inspect the fusible link. The fusible link is the thinnest section of the conductor within the fuse, and it is this which melts when too much current is drawn. Like most fuses, the only real reliability problem this fuse suffers from is corrosion of the terminals. The author once owned a Volvo that had previously had problems with corrosion in the fuse box, demonstrated by a number of the plastic fuses having melted from the heat generated by the poor connection.

When we build a system with redundancy in mind, for example a fuel system incorporating a spare fuel pump, it is important that we consider how these systems are fused. Installing two components with one of these only to be used in the event of failure of the other is known as a 'dual-redundancy' system. Primarily employed on aircraft (where component failure can really ruin your day) dual-redundancy systems are intended to improve the reliability of systems which are either prone to failure, possibly due to the high demands placed upon them, or those which are vital for the safe running of the equipment. In the case of a competition car the reasons for using dual redundancy are more likely to be the former than the latter, although most road cars are equipped with some form of dual-redundancy.

If a headlight circuit burns out on a modern car the other headlamp will continue to operate, even if the first circuit actually burned out its fuse. The reason for this is that the two halves of this same system run two separate fuses, which allows one to

By arranging all the fuses to be placed near the occupants fuse changes 'on-the-fly' are a possibility for the brave. (Peacemarsh Garage)

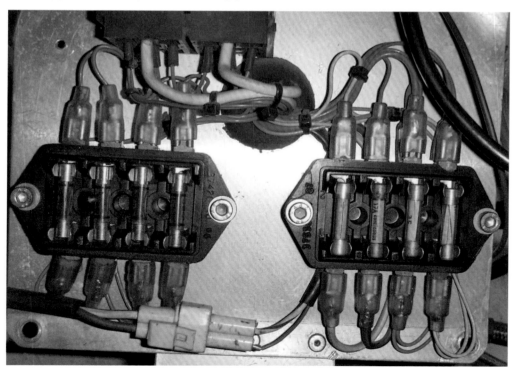

Component reliability is a lot more important when there is no pit-lane to retire to! (PIAA UK)

continue to operate even if the other is damaged. Just how critical this is would be best discovered when travelling at 70mph on a deserted, unlit stretch of dual carriageway in the early hours of the morning.

When a spare fuel pump is fitted for example, it is important that we remember to include not just an extra fuse, but extra wiring to supply it as well – known as duplexing. It makes sense to allow this wiring loom to follow a different route to the component (a process made much easier if your loom already follows more than one path to the rear of the car) as this means that any damage to a section of loom will allow the other pump, which is running from an undamaged section of loom, to operate normally and allow you to get safely to the service area. If we take dual-redundancy to its very simplest form, we could just mount the spare component next to the component in regular use, and in the event of the main component failing simply plumb in the new one using the existing loom. However, this is time consuming, and rather negates the advantages of weight saving that racing teams are so keen on encouraging. It does not really help if the component is not the faulty part of the system either.

So we have discussed our blade-type fuse and how it should be used in the wiring of a competition vehicle. Now as useful as these fuses are, it would be a lot handier if the fuse was not disposable, and could be reused after failure. As a sort of halfway house between the fuse and the circuit breaker comes the self-resetting fuse. This fuse uses the heat produced by too much current being drawn to operate a thermal cut-out rather than melt a wire. When the fuse has cooled down, the thermal cut-out is allowed to reset. If the fault is still present then the fuse will 'pop' again, but if the fault has been cured then the power supply will be restored to normal. This system is useful, but seldom found on competition vehicles; however on some road cars it is employed to prevent damage to electric window mechanisms.

The weapon of choice on competition vehicles is the automotive circuit breaker, or CB. The circuit breakers found on most competition vehicles are identical to those on military and civilian aircraft. Although a lot more expensive than fuses, the versatility of circuit

Design your loom to be versatile; this allows you to compete in more diverse events. (Terry Lawless)

breakers is a definite boon for the competition car driver and crew. During maintenance individual circuits can be isolated; how many times have you needed to spin the engine without it firing up? Isolate the fuel pump supply and you can do this with ease.

Circuit breakers operate in a similar way to fuses: if an over-current situation occurs then the circuit is interrupted. Whilst a fuse does this by burning out an intentional weak link, circuit breakers tend to use a bimetallic strip (two different metals bonded together that bend as they are heated) to throw a switch which isolates the circuit. By pressing the button that protrudes through the panel in which the breaker is mounted the CB can be reset, allowing current to flow again until the next over-current situation. The circuit breakers we use are rather like dashboard icebergs; despite only needing a 10mm hole drilled in the dash they take up a lot more space behind it. However, when circuit breakers are fitted immediately alongside each other, the terminals that supply the power from the battery can be linked with metal bars rather than wires to provide a reliable and strong connection.

CBs are not an ideal solution; for a start, they can cost 50 to 100 times what a single fuse would set you back. They are heavier, and take up more dashboard space than fuses (they are larger behind the dash than they are at the front), and can sometimes 'trip' with no provocation, although with the latest versions this problem is becoming a rarity. It is their versatility that makes them so valuable in the competition car as they can be used to isolate systems while they are worked on, or to disable a faulty component mid-race. They provide an instant visual clue as to which system is at fault, as when they trip the shaft of the breaker protrudes a few millimetres further into the cabin, exposing a white collar to show it has tripped.

Systems which need to be disconnected due to race regulations or similar, can be prevented from being inadvertently operated by tightening a plastic tie-wrap around the shaft of the breaker button. This stops the button from returning to its reset position when pushed, and effectively prevents the circuit from operating until the tie-wrap has been removed.

One of the most valuable properties of the CB, its reusable nature, is probably most useful when building your competition car. When a loom is being created and systems are being tested there are so many variables that even the most conscientious competition car builder can make mistakes. The author once experienced a wiring fault on an exotic factory-prepared Italian sports car racing in a one-make championship series. A resistor, designed to dump the alternator load if the electrical cut-off switch was operated, had been fitted in such a way that if the starting battery was plugged in it would dump all its current across the rubber-mounted components. The first question was: who decided that mounting a resistor (which is designed to get quite hot in use) in a rubber P-clip was a good idea. Secondly, how did this poor wiring design slip through a factory competition car preparation? I discovered this wiring fault after switching off the battery isolator switch having (foolishly) left the booster battery connected. It was only when I noticed the cockpit was full of smoke that I realised there was a problem. If I had gone to lunch before noticing this the results could have been disastrous.

The first time you apply power to a new wiring loom is a nerve-wracking experience and if you can do it without wincing you are braver than I! However, if you have fitted circuit breakers the worst that is likely to happen is the 'pop' of a CB tripping (but don't forget that the length of loom between the CB and the battery could still cause a short circuit if it chafes against the bodywork). If you are using breakers then the offending CB is quickly located, and to fix it is simply a matter of extending your finger to reset it. If a fuse burns out you have to first locate it, which

This wiring appears neat and tidy, although with closer inspection some very tight radii are visible on the injector plugs, which is asking for an internal cable breakdown. (Paul Martin)

can be time consuming, and then replace it with a new one. With a new loom this could happen many times until the fault is found, assuming you have been lucky enough to have just the one fault.

It is possible to cut down the amount of fuses and/or circuit breakers you use by having one fuse/breaker for more than one item. The items using the breaker should be of a similar current draw, and the protection device rated to accept both of these devices when they are operating at full load. As we have seen earlier, using one CB for both circuits on a dual-redundancy system would be foolish, but putting more than one item on a single CB is good planning. There is nothing to say that you need to use one type of circuit protection exclusively and there is a lot to be said for protecting some systems with fuses while using circuit breakers for the more critical items. Items seldom prone to failure could use fuses, while the more temperamental items could rely on a CB. Don't forget the other use of the circuit breaker and that is to isolate systems in a way that is much more convenient than pulling a fuse.

If we were building a rally car there are two extremes of preparation we could take. We could build it along the lines of a Formula One car with added ground clearance and it would be light and fast, but far too fragile. If it were built along the same lines as the Challenger 2 main battle tank then it would be practically indestructible, but too heavy to be anywhere near competitive; even 1,200bhp can't set fast times if it has over 60 tons to haul around! So, to build a competitive rally car we need to find a balance between durability and performance. The same can be said of looming up our competition car.

By mounting relays and fuses within reach of the crew they can be changed on the move when under pressure.

This circuit breaker is currently in the 'tripped' position, and to reset is simply pushed until the white band is hidden. (Peacemarsh Garage)

The cable from the battery to the starter motor is as thick as it is for a reason: it has to carry a lot of current. Cables carrying electronic signals with little current draw are a lot thinner and therefore weigh less. As well as being lighter, thinner cables are more flexible and easier to loom. Selecting cables to suit the loads placed upon them is normally very simple, as cable and component ratings are usually clearly marked. An example of this could be wiring in a radiator fan. The fan chosen for the task has a rating of 12A, and as a general rule is cable rated 30 per cent higher than the expected normal flow to take into account variations in the current drawn. Therefore, 30 per cent of 12A is 3.6A, which gives a total of 15.6A. We then use whichever cable is rated above this figure. Were we to go too high above this figure the wiring will be oversized, although if there is nothing else available there should be no problem with using it. However, we go *below* the figure then the cable will be rated below that of the current being drawn, and could cause a fire, or at the very least, overheating of the loom. You should *never* use cable that is not rated high enough to supply the component you are fitting. Although 30 per cent is the figure I tend to work to, in theory you could drop this threshold to allow you to adopt a smaller cable size, but I have found this allowance has always given an adequate buffer without resulting in oversized cables.

The figure I have quoted for the fan current rating was taken from the manufacturer's details, however if these are not available you can measure the current drawn by using a multimeter in series with the component. Remember that the current drawn will be higher during the start up of the motor, as it takes more current to get it up to speed. Electric heaters also draw more current initially, as an increased amount of energy is required to bring them up to operating temperature than is required to keep them there. Using the highest figure you record under load is the safest bet, and then include the 30 per cent threshold.

Working out the ratings for circuit breakers should always be done with such a threshold in mind; otherwise you run the risk of spending an entire race resetting the CB on a component that is perfectly fine. Sometimes, components are rated in watts instead of amps, in which case you can work out the current rating by simply dividing the wattage by 12V, as this is the voltage all components utilise other than the HT side of the ignition and HID lighting system. For example, if the radiator fan was rated at 140w we would divide 140 by 12, giving a typical current rating of 11.6A. Add on 3.48 to include the 30 per cent threshold and we are given a cable requirement of around 15A – roughly the rating we had decided was suitable for our original fan. If two identical fans are run in parallel then the current rating of all wiring and circuit breakers will need to be doubled to take this into account. In an ideal world we would run two fans with individual wiring and circuit breakers, however this means that all the wiring would have to be duplicated, bumping up the weight. The advantage of course is that in the event of one system failing the other carries on working, unaffected.

Many domestic automatic cars prevent the driver from removing the key from the ignition until the transmission has been placed in 'Park'. This system of accident prevention through interlocks has been carried out for many years in a variety of different ways. Modern smoke alarms are sometimes fitted with a sprung-loaded bar that prevents them from being mounted on the wall unless a battery is present, and microwave ovens cannot be switched on unless the door is locked closed. *Poka-yoke* was a principle of manufacture pioneered by an engineer called Shigeo Shingo, who worked for Toyota streamlining their impressive production process. The general idea behind the *Poka-yoke* concept is that by removing the ability of the operator to make mistakes we remove the possibility of human-error. When you fill your car up with fuel you are prevented from accidentally filling it with the wrong fuel (petrol or diesel) by the use of different-sized nozzles. No matter how many glaringly obvious notices are put up, no matter how many warnings are given, people will still make mistakes.

If we can effectively prevent these mistakes by making them physically impossible then we will save time and money in the long run. Imagine how the driver feels when sitting on the grid, going through one last cockpit familiarisation before he earns his keep. It is easy to be 'on the ball' when the mind is alert and the body is fresh, but an hour into the race when the mind is not really at its best, it can be a different matter. By effectively 'fool-proofing' the cockpit the possibility of mishaps occurring can be reduced. If an electronically controlled gearbox has an interlock that prevents it from being put into reverse accidentally while there is forward road speed then the possibility of 'popping' a 'box due to carelessness is eliminated.

The term fail-safe is wrongly applied if used to define practically any system which is designed to prevent damage to a component. The correct use of the term refers to any component that is designed to default to a certain condition, should it fail. An example of this is the braking system on trains. On a car the brakes need to have hydraulic pressure applied to make them slow the vehicle. In the event of failure we have a back-up braking system in the form of the handbrake, which is why the MoT test dictates the handbrake cannot be hydraulic. The brakes on trains are pneumatically operated, and in the days of steam, used to rely on a vacuum to release them. If the vacuum was not present then the brakes remained firmly on and the train went nowhere. So, in the event of a leak, pipe separation or other braking system failure, the affected systems failed to 'On', applying the train's brakes. The advantages of this were obvious; in the event of a brake failure there will be no runaway carriages

OVERLEAF *Dust can and will get everywhere, causing electrical components to overheat and preventing good connections.* (Theunis du Plessis)

as even if a vehicle broke away from the rest of the train its brakes would be automatically applied the moment the vacuum was lost.

For this reason, when we start wiring up our electrical systems it makes a great deal of sense to set everything up in such a way that if a failure occurs the components affected will default to the safest setting. Modern cars are designed that if the ECU suffers a failure serious enough to cause it to stop operating the system will default to a 'limp-home' mode. This mode dispenses with all the highly polished techniques for getting maximum performance for minimal fuel, and simply sets the ignition timing and fuelling to a default setting that will get the car safely home, albeit at a greatly reduced speed.

Certain types of machinery use a device known as a 'dead-man's handle'. This operates the machinery as long as there is pressure upon it. Should the operator fall asleep or be otherwise diverted from his supervision of the machinery the pressure will be removed from the handle, stopping the machine. A similar device is found on lawnmowers. An advancement of this device has been used on trains, where the driver is required to press a button whenever a buzzer is sounded. This verifies to the machinery that the driver is awake, and should the operator not return the required response the train will automatically apply its brakes and come to a halt. The practical uses for these systems on a competition car are varied, and will only really become apparent as you inspect the systems to see what can be improved upon. Hopefully, this has given you a few ideas to work with.

Chapter 6

Batteries, starting and charging systems

BEFORE WE START on the subject of batteries I feel obliged to state some basic safety measures. Batteries generally contain acid, which will burn skin, eyes, and anything else it touches. In the event of coming in contact with battery acid you should wash the area affected with water mixed with baking soda to neutralise the corrosive action of the electrolyte. If you are unlucky enough to get the electrolyte in your eyes you should gently bathe them with flowing cool water for at least five minutes, and seek medical advice as soon as possible. Should you swallow any battery acid, take an antacid indigestion remedy immediately, seek medical advice, and give yourself a talking to for not being very bright. Lead/acid batteries give off explosive gases in use, and most of all during charging. For this reason it is preferable to keep sources of ignition away from batteries that are being charged. Switch the charger off at the wall before disconnecting the terminals as this reduces the possibility of a spark. Try to charge batteries in a room with good ventilation. It is rare, but not unknown, for a battery to explode during charging so choose your charging place with care. If you need to add electrolyte to a non-sealed type battery, always add the concentrated acid to the water when making up the electrolyte compound, and never the other way around. Eye protection is prudent when working with batteries, and as with all electrical systems, if in doubt, do more research.

The battery is the very heart of the electrical system and modern racing batteries, such as the well-known Varley Red Top range, tend to be of the lead/acid type. Basic lead/acid batteries have been around for a long time; the first believed to have been constructed by Gaston Planté in 1859. Modern racing lead/acid batteries are based upon those which have been used in aircraft for many years. These are usually sealed, allowing them to be mounted in ways that would cause conventional batteries to leak badly. lead/acid batteries consist of a grid cast from a lead alloy, invariably lead/antimony or lead/calcium. Lead/calcium batteries are often considered to be a fairly recent invention although they were being manufactured even before the Second World War.

Calcium batteries have a couple of advantages over antimony batteries, primarily that they are not so prone to losing electrolyte when in use, have a higher grid alloy melting point (which, for reasons we won't bother with here, makes the construction of the battery easier for the manufacturer), and a low self-discharge rate. (In other words, it can hold a charge for a long time if no drain is placed upon it.)

However, it is only recently that manufacturing techniques and improvements in the chemical make-up of the lead/calcium alloy have reduced the tendency of the grids to crack due to a process known as grid growth. Calcium batteries are great for the lower budget competitor to use in racing because of the small amount of gas discharged when in use which allows them to be fully sealed. When a calcium battery becomes fully discharged however, there is a high likelihood of *barrier layer sulphation* occurring, which is where the surface of the grid is transformed into a thick sulphate of lead. This results in the battery becoming harder to recharge, and the final charge the battery is capable of holding becomes greatly reduced. For this reason, great care must be taken to ensure that your expensive racing batteries are never allowed to get into a state of low or total discharge lest they become a heavy acidic lump of scrap. Batteries are normally rated in ampere-hours. Put simply, a battery rated at 50A/h is capable of supplying 50 amps for an hour, or 1 amp for 50 hours (2 amps for 25 hours and so forth). These figures are only intended to give a guideline as to the storage capacity of the cells, as battery performance will depend on the ambient temperature, state of the cells, chemical balance of the electrolyte, and so forth.

A relatively new technique in battery construction uses a glass-fibre mat to soak up the acid. Because this mat is soaked in the acid it can be sandwiched between the lead plates, and rolled up. This creates batteries that look a little like a six-pack of beer when viewed from above. Absorbed glass matt (or AGM) batteries can use lead without antimony and other chemicals added as the lead plates are held firmly in place and do not need to be stiffened. They require less acid to be contained within the battery, and can be fully sealed and self discharge at a lower rate, while boasting a lower internal resistance due to the close proximity of the plates. Racing batteries have been using the AGM technique for some years, allowing the size of the battery to be

The battery should be mounted as low as possible to keep the centre of gravity low down. (Wren Classics)

kept compact. Not surprisingly, this means racing batteries are more expensive than their non-race counterparts. A racing battery may be more efficient than a domestic type, which means you could drop down in size with no compromise in performance. Comparing the road-spec battery with the race spec and you may be surprised at how much weight and space you can save.

Another type of lead/acid battery uses an electrolyte that has been thickened to a paste, referred to as Gel type batteries. This is to remove the problem of having acid flowing around the cells when the battery is moved or has accelerative forces applied to it. AGM batteries get around this problem by cutting down on the amount of acid used and holding it in suspension, so combine this with the other advantages that the AGM type has and Gel batteries rapidly become a less attractive option.

Whatever the type of battery it needs to be secured firmly, and if within the passenger cell boxed in a vented container designed to minimise the risk of electrolyte spillage should the battery become damaged. Vent tubes coming from this casing should be piped in such a way that any fluids coming from the battery are not vented into the passenger cell. For further information, check the MSA regulations with reference to the formula you are entering, as they are likely to be quite strict on the subject (and quite rightly so; acid burns are nasty). Normally the boxes used are manufactured from glass-fibre and are mounted on the floor.

When placing a battery in the cockpit various questions have to be asked such as; where will the weight of the battery be of the most use to me, and could it be used to counteract the driver's weight by being placed in the passenger side footwell? Many hill-climb single-seaters mount the battery directly under the driver's legs, which is a position I don't think I would be very comfortable with! However, as most hill-climbers use a total loss system (in other words rely on the charge within the battery to run the engine and minimal electrics without using an on-board generator system) there is less risk of the battery doing anything nasty. A majority of the exciting battery failures happen when it is being charged, either on the bench or by the vehicle charging system. Therefore a total loss system presents less of a risk to the driver if the battery is placed nearby as it is not being charged when racing.

Remember that the longer the wiring the more losses will be encountered, so try to mount the battery near to the components that require maximum power from it. The starter motor is one of these components and you may find that it labours quite badly when powered by a battery that has a long cable linking the two. With situations such as these, and any situation where you wish to run as small a battery as possible the use of a boost battery can be considered. These batteries are mounted on small hand trolleys to enable them to be moved up to the vehicle with a minimum of effort. When alongside the competition car a pair of short, heavy duty current leads are attached to the battery terminals and terminate in a connector designed to carry large currents. These terminals are usually like those used to charge forklift trucks and the like, and should be relatively cheaply available from motor factors which deal with heavy goods vehicles.

Known as Anderson connectors, these are quick to connect and capable of flowing large quantities of current due to the large size of the terminals. When we wish to start the car or leave it running for any length of time (in a total loss system) we simply connect the boost battery allowing the vehicle to drain power from the large trolley-mounted battery rather than its own modest supply. By doing this we can radically reduce the size of the battery we need to carry on board, but be aware that most regulations insist that the vehicle is still able to be restarted mid-race using its own internal battery should a stall occur.

As this is a scenario which is unlikely to happen a lot we can really get close to the

OPPOSITE *This is a fairly normal place to mount the battery in a single-seater. Make sure it is undamaged before every use; battery acid on the legs is rather unpleasant!* (Paul Martin)

ABOVE *Using an external battery to start means you can reduce the size of the internal battery, or even dispense with it entirely.* (Paul Martin)

absolute minimum weight of battery that needs to be carried. The downside with this is that the smaller the battery the more likely it is to be damaged by having to start a large capacity, high-compression race engine. For teams with a large budget this is a risk they can take; for a more modestly financed racer it is probably worth going for safety with a slightly larger set of cells that are more likely to recover after a few mid-race starts.

According to the regulations set out by the MSA for almost all forms of racing, a battery cut-off switch is required. If we were to just fit a high-current switch between the battery and the car, then any engine with an alternator is likely to keep running; remember that the battery is primarily there to start the car, and once running the alternator supplies the electrical power. For this reason MSA-approved master switches have a high-current switch with an extra set of low-current contacts mounted below. In normal use these contacts are set with one set closed and the other open. The closed contacts allow power to the ignition to allow the engine to run, while the open set is connected to a resistor, normally about 3 ohms and 13 watts. This dumps the current in the system straight to earth through the loading of the resistor when the switch is set to 'off' and is so designed to prevent the alternator from trying to supply power to the circuit by discarding it. So when the switch is operated the main terminals open, disconnecting the battery, one set of small terminals open, shutting off the ignition, and the last set of terminals closes which dumps the power on the engine side of the master switch to earth via a load.

Where possible, the boost battery needs to be connected on the battery side of this switch so that if the switch is operated in the pit-lane or workshop with the boost battery connected the car is still isolated. If it is mounted the other side of the switch then the current dumping resistor will try to discard the entire current supplied by the boost battery, which could get messy. Make sure the resistor is mounted in a way that isolates it from the car, yet allows it to get hot with no damage to its surroundings. If you think this sounds like the voice of experience, then you may be right!

A compromise has to be found between keeping the wiring short and ensuring that the cut-off is within easy reach of the driver. As you are usually required to have a method of isolation both inside and outside of the vehicle the easiest way is to mount the isolator within the passenger cell, such as on the transmission tunnel, and then use a pull cable fitted with a T-handle to operate it from outside of the car. Usually mounted at the base of the windscreen, this handle should be clearly marked with the MSA-approved lightning bolt symbol, and should be placed next to the T-handle or button which operates the fire extinguisher, also clearly marked. Try to ensure there can be no confusion as to which handle operates which item; it will ruin your day if some kind-hearted person intends to kill the battery, but instead deploys the extinguisher into the cockpit and engine bay.

If you are using a cable to operate the isolator switch then it is unlikely that the key will ever stray too far from the switch. The keys used to operate these isolator switches are fairly universal, so don't be tempted to use them as a sole security measure. Losing the key at a critical time could really make life difficult, so if it is not already attached use some cord or wire to connect it to the switch or bodywork around it. Obviously this cord should not interfere with the movement of the key, and should allow the key to be fully removed, not just turned off. The reason for this is

By fabricating a small trolley for this battery our lives could be simplified (and back muscles spared!). (Paul Martin)

that the removal of the key provides a useful visual cue that the power has been isolated from the vehicle, allowing you to work around the engine in relative safety. If you are carrying out electrical work on the car then a blanking cap could be placed over the isolator key hole warning others that applying power could prove dangerous due to unfinished wiring, or similar.

When it comes to choosing an alternator do not immediately discard the stock unit. Despite the fact that the standard alternator found in a family hatchback has been designed to supply heavy loads such as electric windows, it should not be discarded simply because these items have been removed. The amount of horsepower that an alternator drains from an engine is largely dependent on the electrical load placed upon it. In a stripped racing saloon these loads are minimal, so the drain on the engine is also small. Also, the pulley on the alternator can be increased in size to allow it to spin at a slower speed with relation to the engine. For the average family car the ability to run all the electrical items and maintain battery charge while stationary in traffic is important. Our race machine is seldom sat at idle, uses the top half of the rev-range far more often than the cooking hatchback, and has less equipment to run (complete with a smaller battery to charge). Therefore running a larger pulley will run the alternator slower, dragging less power from the engine. It will be at its optimum charging speed at higher engine rpm (useful in a race engine), and less prone to failure. All in all it would appear to be a worthwhile modification. If you choose to manufacture your own pulley, bear in mind that the material used will have to maintain its structural integrity at the engine's maximum speed (and should be

Ensure there is plenty of airflow to the alternator; excess heat can drastically shorten their life. (Elliott Russell)

rated far beyond this for safety), and that you will need to fit a longer belt to avoid running out of adjustment. Of course, this pulley modification could be applied to other engine-driven ancillaries to liberate more power from the engine but be certain to check they can still operate effectively at their new, lower speed first.

Driving the alternator can be achieved through a number of different techniques; the most common on modern production cars being the poly-vee drive belt. Sometimes known as a serpentine drive due to the complicated path they have to travel, the poly-vee drive belt is reliable and rarely slips. However, it can be complicated to replace a failed one if it is driving a lot of components. If an automatic tensioner is used the replacement process is simply a matter of holding back the tensioner while the new belt is manoeuvred into place. Once the new belt is in place the tensioner can be gently released, which automatically applies the correct tension to the belt. The whole process is very simple, assuming the number of pulleys is low, but on a complicated engine the installer is required to grow at least three extra hands to keep the belt located until the tensioner can be released.

Some race engines use a toothed drive belt similar to a cam belt, the advantage of which is that you can be certain none of the components is suffering a loss of drive due to belt slip. The disadvantage of this system is that the pulleys required are very hard to make for the competitor on a budget, and an aftermarket kit will almost

OPPOSITE *This Classic Jaguar uses vee-belts to drive its ancillaries; these days poly-vee belts have proven more reliable and require less maintenance.* (Wren Classics)

BELOW *This starter motor is a lightweight geared variant, more expensive than normal road trim, but lighter and drawing less current.*

certainly have to be purchased, including not only the belt but all the pulleys required to drive the components required.

The starter motors supplied with road cars are more than adequate for the job they are required to do. Assuming the under-bonnet layout keeps the motor away from life-shortening influences such as exhaust manifold heat and oil, they have a long life; they are not flawless however. Due to the very nature of the task they have to perform they are heavy and have a high current drain, two characteristics we try to avoid in motorsport components. However, a competition-spec starter motor is lighter, more compact, cranks faster and uses less current. This is achieved by using a motor that spins much faster than a standard one, and is then geared down to a speed that will give it enough torque to turn the engine over.

These starter motors are a great little investment, and often weigh as little as 3kg. The disadvantage (there had to be one) is the price. Competition starter motors are more expensive, largely due to the gearing needed. It is for this reason that most standard road cars are not fitted with this type as standard. One great advantage of the compact size of such starter motors is the increased space afforded to nearby components, the exhaust being a good example. Competition exhausts tend to be of a larger bore and follow a different route to standard systems, sometimes right by the starter. The proximity of the exhaust can have a detrimental affect on the life of the motor, and bearing in mind the price we have paid for our competition unit, we really need to do something to maximise its life. For around £30 it is possible to buy heat shielding material designed specifically to shroud the starter motor and when the outlay is so small the advantages are immediately obvious.

Chapter 7

Ignition systems

BEFORE I GO into any depth on the subject of ignition systems, let me stress that this chapter is not designed to replace the work that many others have carried out in the past in writing definitive volumes on engine management and such like. Programming ECUs has undoubtedly become simpler, cheaper and more accessible these days, but the techniques tend to differ depending on the system in use. Because of this I am going to focus more on the components of the ignition system, and leave the ECU wizardry to the likes of Dave Walker, the ECU guru.

Whilst there are quite a few different types of spark ignition systems the principles they share are very similar. If we divide the systems into sections they become much easier to understand. First of all we need a device to generate a high-voltage spark. Most ignition systems use one or two coils connected to the spark plugs by high tension (HT) leads. These leads are insulated with a very thick elastic coating, usually silicon or similar, which prevents the spark from being grounded before it has reached the plug. Older designs use one coil which sends its spark to a unit which distributes it to the cylinder that is at the power stroke of the combustion cycle, a device which is of course called the distributor.

Newer designs consist of a coil pack to which all the plug leads are connected. This coil pack sends the sparks directly to the required cylinders without the intervention of a distributor, which obviously increases reliability. A few manufacturers, such as Alfa Romeo, sometimes dispense with HT leads entirely, preferring to give each spark plug its own coil mounted directly on the plug. The advantages with this include the removal of the resistances and unreliability that an HT lead introduces, and more time for each coil to charge between sparks (as the coil is only required to provide one spark every two revolutions of the engine). Most manufacturers use the coil pack however, as one coil pack per engine instead of one coil pack per cylinder keeps manufacturing costs down to a reasonable level without compromising performance. Four-cylinder engine coil packs normally have three terminals, which may seem strange bearing in mind there are four spark plugs to fire. The answer is found when we discover that the coil pack uses a technique called wasted spark. This system uses one coil shared between two cylinders. When the coil is fired the spark goes not only to the cylinder which is on the power stroke, but also to the cylinder on its exhaust stroke. This spark serves no purpose (although in theory it could assist in the combustion of unburnt fuel) and has no effect on the running of the engine. However, it does reduce the complexity of the ignition system by allowing you to halve the number of coils required. These coil packs tend to be mounted on the bulkhead of the vehicle, or on a bracket on the engine. The best installations are situated close to the spark plugs, reducing the length of the HT leads, which in turn reduces the drop in

This coil pack is one of a pair fitted to a racing V8 TVR. One is used for each bank of cylinders.

spark ferocity. Before systems such as these were employed manufacturers used some ingenious techniques for maximising the spark delivered to the engine.

During starting the starter motor takes the vast majority of the current from the battery, leaving barely enough to run the other systems on the car. For this reason most ignition switches turn off luxuries such as radio and heater fan for the brief

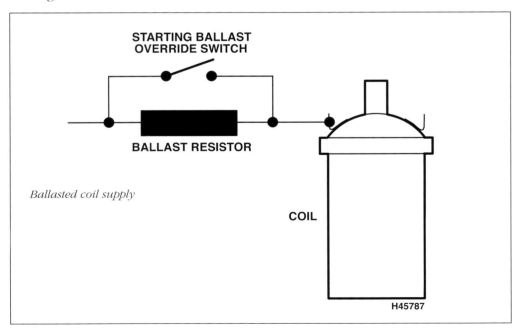

Ballasted coil supply

moment that the key is turned to start the engine to allow the current to be more effectively utilised where required most. As the voltage supplied to the ignition components could drop by a few volts during starter motor operation the ballasted coil came into use. This is designed to run at a much lower voltage than the normal battery/alternator set-up would supply. To make sure that this voltage is achieved a 'ballast resistor' is used. The resistor is fitted in series in the power supply to the coil, and ensures that in normal operation the coil receives approximately half the battery voltage. This means that the coil is designed to operate and produce its optimum spark at around six volts, and gives an equivalent spark to a 12V system. On starting the car a switch operates which effectively bypasses the resistor, supplying the coil with unballasted battery voltage. As the starter motor is operating at this time the battery voltage is less anyway, so bypassing the resistor means that although the coil is operating at a much higher voltage than it would during normal operation, it is not anywhere near 12V. This slightly increased voltage supply means a slightly stronger spark than usual, which is ideal during cold starting.

It is important to make sure you fit the right coil for your vehicle as whilst a ballast type coil would produce a strong spark if run continuously at 12V its life would be very limited. If a non-ballast coil was run on a system using a ballast resistor the coil would only be supplied with half its required voltage, and would not operate correctly. Either way, the results are pretty undesirable, and the importance of checking you are using the right components is vital.

A system which uses yet another type of coil is CDI, which stands for capacitor discharge ignition, and the name is derived from the use of a capacitor to feed the coil. To do this the capacitor needs to be charged to over 300 volts before being triggered. When triggered by the system the capacitor dumps the charge it has gained directly into the ignition coil primary winding. By using this high primary voltage we can create a short duration but very high intensity spark, this technique creating consistently high power sparks which in turn mean better combustion in the cylinder. As it requires less charging time between pulses than a normal coil system we can create more sparks in a given time frame. The knock-on effect of this is that we can use this ignition system in higher revving engines with no reduction in spark intensity at high rpm. The coils used in the CDI systems differ from those used in other ignition systems due to the low inductance of the primary coil. This allows the capacitor to discharge rapidly, which it could not do swiftly enough with a normal coil. One disadvantage of this system is the requirement for over 300 volts to be present to charge the capacitor to the voltage needed. This is usually carried out by using an inverter. In an alternator we use a rectifier to convert ac into dc that we can use in our 12Vdc vehicle; an inverter does the opposite. We need to convert the dc into ac as we generate the higher voltage by means of a transformer. Once the transformer has converted the low voltage into a higher voltage the ac is rectified back into dc to charge the capacitor.

Up to now we have discussed some of the types of coil available; the techniques for triggering these various types of coil are even more varied. Almost unbelievably the simplest techniques are often the ones that people are most afraid of. Modern cars utilise an ECU (electronic control unit) to decide exactly when the injectors should fire, how much fuel should be injected, and crucially to us, when the coil or coils should fire. As the ECU controls all advance and retardation of the timing we no longer have to worry about complicated mechanisms contained within distributors. A simple sensor detecting holes, slots or teeth in a rotating wheel gives the ECU the basic information it needs to sort out the ignition timing. A missing tooth or slot widened to cover two holes or similar informs the ECU about the position of the piston (for example by pinpointing the position of top dead centre) and gives the ECU rpm information for its own use and to drive other items such as the tacho. The Ford Zetec engine uses a sensor mounted in the block picking up holes drilled in the back of the flywheel, while the Vauxhall 'Red Top' uses a grooved wheel mounted on the crankshaft within the block. As mentioned, all timing calculations are carried out electronically and therefore require no other mechanical compensation.

The most widely used method of triggering the coil before the advent of electronic ignition systems was the contact breaker points system. Simply a cam-operated switch, this system is simple and reliable, assuming it is kept well maintained. Periodically the points (contacts of the switch) need to be cleaned, and inspected for erosion. They should be adjusted to ensure the correct gap is being maintained when they are open, which can be a little fiddly when hampered by a whacking great pair of twin-choke carbs. To improve the reliability of this system a hybrid of the electronic and mechanical triggering systems made its debut.

Originally available as a kit to upgrade older points type systems (and still commercially available) this was a unit that utilised a sensor in the place of the points, and a 'chopper' in the place of the cam. When the chopper entered the proximity of the sensor it interrupted a beam of light, which used a basic transistor amplifier to switch the coil on and off. Variations of this technique became available, including a similar system using a magnetic field instead of a light beam. These systems meant low maintenance combined with the simplicity of the points system. Some of the more compact systems fit entirely within the distributor, meaning that the driver of a classic car can upgrade their ignition without having to fit ugly boxes into their standard-looking engine bay.

Hall effect triggering shares a similar principle, but instead of interrupting a magnetic field the Hall effect unit generates a magnetic pulse as it passes the sender, in much the same way that an alternator does. These systems have the advantage that they are not badly affected by the presence of dirt or grime on the sensors, a problem which was known to affect the optical type of trigger. As these systems just take the place of the original points system the vacuum controlled and centrifugal advance and retard is retained if present.

A great deal of people preparing race engines using distributors, such as the drivers of pre-BMW Minis, remove the vacuum advance set-up and upgrade the centrifugal advance to suit. Basically, the vacuum advance system alters the timing to take into account the load placed on the engine by moving the plate on which the points sit. As the points are moved back and forth their position with relation to the cam alters, meaning they are triggered either earlier or later (hence the term advance or retard). On a road engine this makes the engine more drivable and flexible, which is why some tuners find the procedure of removing it for racing rather strange. The centrifugal system also advances and retards the ignition timing, but is based purely on the rpm of the engine. This is carried out by the use of centrifugal weights within the base of the distributor, acting on the points base in the same way that the vacuum system does. Combined with the vacuum system this makes for a flexible way of controlling the ignition timing to produce smooth power delivery without pre-detonation.

In modern cars this entire process takes place electronically and with great accuracy within the ECU. One of the great advantages with the ECU system is the sheer number of parameters it can take into account when running the engine. Aside from utilising the temperature of the outside air and water in the radiator when setting fuelling and timing, it can even make adjustments to parameters such as the idle speed when the

OPPOSITE *No matter what vintage the engine, modern ECU and coil set-ups can have a great impact on performance and drivability.* (Paul Martin)

battery voltage gets low, to assist the alternator with charging. Of course, extra parameters to measure means more sensors to fit (and theoretically to fail), but after running this type of system for a short time the advantages become obvious. For example most modern fuel injection engines are fitted with a knock sensor. This device consists of a crystal mounted within a plastic casing which is bolted directly to the block. In the event of 'pinking', otherwise known as detonation, the crystal picks up the vibration generated and gives off a voltage.

The voltage signal is used by the ECU as a warning that detonation has occurred, which causes it to retard the ignition timing until the problem stops. In this manner the engine can make up for the use of lower octane fuel for example. The more advanced systems actually make experimental tests while the engine is running to see how far advanced the ignition can run before detonation occurs, and then runs the timing at just before this point. This means the engine is constantly running at the optimum timing for high power output, and automatically uses the extra flexibility that the use of a higher octane fuel allows it. This goes some way to explaining why certain engines seem to notice the effect of higher octane fuel more than others, and removes the requirement to make constant manual adjustments to the timing to make the best use of the fuel available.

Although the components mentioned above are pretty critical for the running of the engine, they are nowhere near as important as the often forgotten heroes of our ignition system: the spark plugs. Spark plugs happily operate between 300° and 700°C with little or no maintenance required. There are hundreds of different types, with various performance varieties available from specialist manufacturers, in a bewildering variety of sizes and heat ratings. Ideally, the face of the threaded section of the plug should sit flush with the head, as too much protrusion could result in contact with the piston, or at the very least would overheat due to their distance from the heat sink qualities afforded by the metal of the head. Too little protrusion would shield the spark from doing its job within the combustion chamber, resulting in poor running.

Plugs can be rated 'hotter' or 'colder', but great care must be taken when using this terminology. A cold plug is one that can pass its heat into the metal of the cylinder head with great efficiency, meaning it is suitable for use in engines where the performance is high and thus generating a lot of heat. A hot plug is one that does not radiate quite so much heat into the block, keeping the tip temperature at a high enough level to maintain efficiency in a fairly unstressed or low power engine. We have to maintain a certain temperature at the tip otherwise carbon and other deposits would coat it and not be burned away, having a detrimental effect on the spark. If the tip is allowed to maintain too high a temperature then it will ignite the fuel/air mixture too soon, causing detonation. Using this information we can base our plug selection on how badly we are being affected by these factors. For example, if plug fouling is occurring with correct mixture and good bore condition etc, the plug could be swapped for one with a slightly hotter heat rating.

Different manufacturers use different methods for expressing their heat ratings, and the lack of standardisation can be very frustrating. As a general rule, outside of America plugs are rated hotter as the heat rating in the plug code drops, while American plugs do the opposite. Champion is one company that uses the American system, but it is not as simple as it may at first appear, as they use their own numbering system which does not follow these rules to the letter. It is best to speak to the manufacturers themselves for information on their specific brand system.

The tip of the spark plug contains the electrode which produces the spark. Modern plugs tend to use some pretty exotic sounding materials for these electrodes, so what are the advantages? Normal plugs used to have an iron centre electrode with a small amount of nickel mixed in to slow down the erosion they suffer when in use. Platinum seems to be a metal of choice in the manufacture of centre electrodes, so why is this better than the iron-nickel type? Sparks can be generated more easily from a small pointed electrode, but we have to maintain a certain thickness to prevent the electrode from burning away in the combustion process. Platinum allows us to use a much thinner electrode without this risk.

One type of plug, called a surface discharge plug, does not resemble a normal spark plug: the face of the plug is flat, and it sits virtually flush with the inside of the combustion chamber. The electrode is surrounded by an insulator, which is surrounded by the body of the plug. As the distance between the body and the centre electrode is the same on all sides it is much less likely to foul, however it is only really suitable for use in CDI systems as the voltage required to make the spark bridge the gap is quite high for exactly the same reason that a platinum plug needs a lower voltage to make the spark. A platinum plug has a small electrode, while a surface discharge plug has a large surface to the electrode.

Some modern plugs form a hybrid of the surface discharge and single electrode plugs. By using more than one ground electrode the spark has more paths it can take, which means that electrode fouling takes place at a much slower rate and has less consequence when it does occur as the spark has alternative routes to travel. Another method used to reduce the effects of fouling is the placement of an air gap within the insulator breaking the conductivity of the centre electrode. This break means the spark has a gap to jump before it gets to the plug. The spark has to be a certain voltage before it can jump this gap, meaning that the spark that reaches the electrode tip starts off at a higher potential than if we had let the potential build up slowly by connecting it directly. This gives the effect of a CDI system, so it doesn't really give any advantage when used with CDI.

Sometimes you may notice a brown-coloured haze around the base of the insulator on the spark plug. It can be wrongly assumed that this is caused by combustion gases seeping up between the insulator and the metal body of the plug. The actual reason behind it is a lot more interesting. Engine bays by their very nature are oily places, even those that look quite clean. Air ejected from the various gaps in the engine seals will contain minute particles of oil, which are attracted to the field generated by the ionized particles which are present at a point of large electrical discharge. These particles occur when a small amount of spark (not normally enough to have an adverse effect on combustion) leaps over the surface of the insulator. Not only does this attract the oil particles in the air, but causes them to discolour when this minor sparking continues. Generally, this 'corona stain' causes no problems, as the oil does not conduct the spark. However, damp or dirty plugs can cause the spark to leap to earth before it comes anywhere near the combustion chamber, which would mean a massive power loss. To prevent this, the plugs need to be kept clean, and inspected frequently to ensure they stay this way.

When setting the gap on a spark plug, consider that the manufacturer's recommended setting assumes that the gap will remain unchecked for some time after the fitment of the plugs. As we are putting a lot more maintenance into our vehicles it makes sense that we can put a larger gap on the plugs, as we will notice the point at which the gap becomes too large due to wear much sooner than the average domestic driver. Most people use feeler gauges for setting spark gaps, the only problem with this technique is that the electrodes never wear flat, but rather erode at the points that the spark travels between. The wire type of plug setting tool is far more accurate. Modern ignition systems produce a much more powerful spark than the points-driven systems of years ago, especially at low rpm, so if you have uprated an older system you could safely increase the spark plug gap. But why would you want to do that? A bigger gap means a larger voltage is required to cross it, which means that when the spark does jump the gap it is at a higher voltage and ferocity. The knock on effect of this is a more aggressive ignition of the fuel/air mixture.

A lot of people are aware of the different types of plug mating face, and that these require a different fitting technique. Plugs which use a conical seat at the top of their threads need to be tightened in by hand as far as they will go until resistance is felt, and then tightened by a further 15°. Plugs with a flat seat and a crush washer use the same technique, but with a 90° tightening at the end. *However,* something most people do not realise is that once this type of plug has been fitted, the crush washer has been deformed to fit the seat, and it does not need 90 degree tightening again. Instead, only 15° is needed to reseat it, and any further could strip the threads from the head. Alloy heads are made from a softer material than the older cast iron type, and are much more susceptible to this happening.

In an ideal world we would replace this crush washer after every removal, but this is not realistically going to happen. Various techniques have been advocated over the years for fitting spark plugs without cross-threading them, in other words, trying to screw them in when they are not perfectly aligned, which can cause very expensive thread damage. One of the most touted methods involves slipping a length of hosepipe over the plug so that applied friction is lost long before thread damage occurs. I always believed this technique to be overkill until multivalve overhead camshaft engines became popular, and spark plugs became recessed ever further into the rocker covers. The best technique for preventing cross threading is to *take your time* refitting the plugs.

Careful securing of these HT leads has improved the potential for reliability considerably.

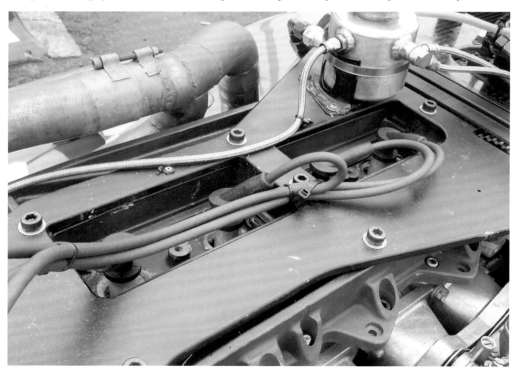

Don't just aimlessly spin the plug on its seat until the thread bites; take the effort to line up the plug with the bore of the hole. If this is done correctly the plug will be aligned to engage the thread straight away, minimising the damage. Sadly, as cylinder heads tend to be made of aluminium alloy the spark plug is much tougher than the material it is screwed in to. So which is going to get damaged if care is not taken: the £10 spark plug or the £1,000 head? It pays to take care when doing this seemingly simple task.

There are a myriad of spark plug leads available on the market; most of the saleability of these items seems to depend on how garish the colour scheme is. If your desire for upgrading your engine extends beyond colour coding it, just how much will a plug lead do for you?

First, we must confirm that we are fully aware of the responsibilities of the plug (or HT) leads. The HT leads must convey the spark with as small a loss as is possible. If the HT lead is too resistive then will the power of the spark be greatly decreased? Most high-quality HT leads in fact have a high resistance to minimise interference without negatively affecting the quality of the spark. They can get away with this because high voltages travel *around* the conductor in a magnetic field rather than down the core. Whilst some wires marketed as low resistance may seem like an investment all they actually offer is lower resistance to radio frequency interference, or RFI, which is a definite disadvantage.

Many of the 'performance' leads on the market boast specialist materials intended either to carry the spark more efficiently (even including claims of boosting the spark are made – a nice trick if you can do it) or to insulate it from losses more effectively. Some claim to have better control over RFI, while others just have their snazzy colour

Keeping the leads as short as possible means a stronger spark.

PREVIOUS PAGE *Rally cars are not always this clean; how reliable will your ignition be when coated liberally with mud?* (Elliott Russell)

scheme to tempt the buyer. One website the author discovered mentioned that cars running a higher than average boost pressure on their turbochargers actually make it more difficult for the spark to jump the gap in the plug due to the cylinder being more crowded. There may be some basis on this theory in physics, but it pays to maintain a healthy degree of scepticism.

The biggest advantages touted by the more reputable of the lead manufacturers are improved resistance to RFI and electromagnetic interference, or EMI. This is more than likely a fair and justifiable claim, and if you require an improvement in RFI/EMI resistance then feel free to upgrade, but for the most part, fancy HT leads are in the author's opinion a waste of money.

However good the HT lead you are not going to see an increase in horsepower, no matter how many precious metals, fancy conductors and pretty colour schemes the makers include. Car manufacturers don't like to spend money without having to, and if this means your plug leads have to miss out on having the latest, greatest compound of silicon in the insulation, then so be it. On the other hand, they would not skimp cost on any item that could cause poor running on your vehicle (especially within the warranty period) so there are some places that they are going to use the most suitable part for the job. Uprating your plug leads can be a good idea from the point of view of reliability, but the author is sceptical about the massive power gains claimed by some companies.

Just like buying spark plugs, the best technique is to assess what is available with eyes wide open and your inner cynic on full alert. While on the subject of plug leads, recent advances in HT lead manufacture have resulted in some unusual faults occurring. For many years the porcelain insulators used on spark plugs have had three or so ribs along their length to increase their resistance to tracking (where the spark travels over the outside of the plug rather than down the centre terminal). These days, as leads have become better insulated some manufacturers have started leaving these grooves out. Since this development a rare problem with leads popping off during running has started to manifest itself. Due to the excellent sealing properties of silicone the newer HT boots are actually sealing air within the boot, which as the spark plug heats up to running temperature expands, creating a high positive pressure. This can cause the plug lead to pop off, leaving you running on one less cylinder than before. Apparently, the cure is to place the boot on to the plug with the closed end pinched to displace as much air as possible. Once in place the boot can be manipulated to displace further air, and the problem should not reoccur.

One thing to bear in mind is that whilst it is an excellent insulator, silicone is not resistant to many of the corrosive chemicals present within the engine bay. For example, battery acid can ruin an expensive set of leads in a very short time indeed. Buying single plug leads is not all that easy so the whole lot have to be replaced if this occurs. Sometimes spark plug cables can be damaged by the inexperienced removing the plug caps while the engine is hot. When hot the terminals on the tops of the plugs expand due to thermal expansion, and lock themselves more securely into the boot. *Never* pull on the wire to remove an HT lead, but always on the boot, as close to the terminal as possible. If you try to remove an HT lead that is firmly held in place by an expanded plug terminal you may find yourself looking forlornly at the bare end of an HT lead and a smug looking HT boot stuck limpet-like to the spark plug.

When choosing the position of the coil the ideal place is as close to the plugs as possible to keep the leads as short as you can, cutting down resistive losses. If a distributor system is used then the coil should be placed as close to the distributor as possible. Sadly, we are rarely at liberty to move the distributor, but the least we can do is keep the king lead short. At first sight the HT leads are slightly misleading, as they appear to carry some high currents due to their diameter. As they are in fact just carrying low amperage high voltage pulses the conductor is in fact very small in diameter. A large amount of the thickness of the lead is taken up by the insulation. This is usually silicone or similar, and is designed to be thick enough to prevent the current from arcing to earth until it reaches the spark plug terminal. For this reason it is important that the HT lead is supported properly; anywhere that it can chafe on sharp metallic edges gives the potential for running the engine on less cylinders than it should do.

An HT lead must also prevent the current it is carrying from generating RFI. This is the cause of whining tones on in-car radio and communications systems, and can even affect the ECU and other electrical components by interfering with them. For this reason it is best to mount the ECU a fair distance from the ignition coil and leads. It is preferable to put the ECU in the passenger compartment, where not only is it shielded from the weather but boasts a large metal bulkhead to screen it from the fields generated by the ignition system. Electrical systems which could be sensitive to high voltage pulses are best kept away from all the high-tension ignition components and this even includes the wiring.

The principle behind the operation of the ignition coil is the generation of voltage in a coil of wire by pulsing a voltage through another coil placed next to it. This pulsing creates a continuously expanding and collapsing field which will in turn induce a voltage into the unpowered coil, which has more turns and therefore multiplies the voltage (at the expense of current) into something high enough to create a spark. In the same way a field is generated by any wire carrying pulsed current, which can induce an unwanted voltage into any wires that may run nearby. The upshot of this is that any wire that runs alongside the HT leads is likely to have an unwanted voltage induced into it which could cause problems in the ECU, instruments or other electrical systems. Don't run ECU leads anywhere near the HT leads; your bank balance will thank you for it!

Chapter 8

Lighting systems

It is fairly obvious that the complexity of the lighting system on a competition car depends a great deal on the type of racing you are doing. Some forms of motorsport are very strict on what lighting can be carried; even 12-car road rallies employ some very tight rulings on the matter. With the average single-seater the only lighting required might be the rain light, in which case there is not a lot of point in you reading this chapter in too much depth! For the rally driver on the other hand, the sheer quantity of types of system is staggering, varying from 100W not-quite-road-legal driving light bulbs to many thousands of pound's worth of high intensity discharge (HID) systems. The competitor really should think very carefully before parting with hard-earned money for equipment such as this. At the budget end of the market certain lighting systems are described in a somewhat misleading manner, and certain on-line auction sites are filled with adverts for 'HID lighting systems' that are no more than standard headlight bulbs with a near useless tint. As usual, *caveat emptor* applies. As the most prolific use of supplementary lighting is rallying this chapter primarily concerns those who like getting cold and muddy.

When fitting extra lighting to a road/rally car then it is necessary to make sure that the extra lamp bowls are firmly mounted in place. It is very distracting to have wobbling beams while hurtling between trees at eye-watering speeds, and it is totally unnecessary as the solution is so simple. By mounting a small arm to the top of the lamp unit and connecting it to a solid part of the front panel it will be prevented from tilting or vibrating excessively. Make sure you don't mount the support arm to a part of the body that may prevent the removal of the grill or similar item at the service stage. This support arm is best constructed in a similar manner to a track rod end, but on a much smaller scale; a threaded bar with a ball joint on the ends.

If you have trouble finding something suitable, then consider visiting a hobby shop. Radio-controlled aircraft utilise threaded rods with small ball joint cups at each end, and the balls that sit in these cups usually come with a threaded stub and are ideal for mounting on an auxiliary light unit. Be sure to purchase materials substantial enough to steady the lamp unit without popping off when the car is vibrating around at speed. Alternatively mounting the lamps in a pod unit is very secure, and if a good quality connector is used it can also be very easy to remove when not needed, assuming you install it with easy removal in mind.

Simply using higher wattage bulbs in existing headlamps is a possibility, but some things need to be considered. First, check the legal maximum wattage allowed by the country in question. Falling foul of the law can dramatically shorten your rally. Secondly, check that the wiring to the headlamps is capable of supplying the extra current that the beefier lamps will require. Not heeding this rule will shorten your rally

This inventive road-rally competitor modified Transit headlight washer jets to suit his Rover 200 rally car. (Clive Chapman)

This rain light has been expertly mounted using a custom bracket.

even more abruptly than the long arm of the law. Thirdly, consider the cooling of the lamp unit. When high-wattage bulbs are used in auxiliary light units hung from the front of the car they tend to have excellent airflow around them, which means the light unit and filament lamp inside keep relatively cool (by bulb standards anyway). With a higher wattage bulb fitted in a standard headlamp the only surface really receiving airflow is the front face. The upshot of this is that the temperature within the headlamp unit is higher, which could mean the bulb life is shortened quite dramatically. Some of the plastics present inside the headlamp unit may have been designed to withstand the heat generated by a 55w bulb but not much more, and an increased temperature here could mean these plastics become damaged, although the likelihood of this is small.

Avoid using auxiliary lighting when not required; quite aside from the unwarranted drain on the charging circuit, the lighting units will become much hotter when the vehicle is stationary and deprived of cooling airflow. You should be able to control each separate lighting system attached to your vehicle. This means that in the event of a system becoming damaged (by being smashed, waterlogged or incapacitated in some way) it can be isolated. Some types of rally require you to extinguish extra lighting when going through areas which are delicate with regards to public relations. This means your auxiliary lighting switch needs to be clearly marked and easy to operate in a hurry. Your lighting is normally going to be required at night, so make the switchgear clear and unambiguous to allow for easy operation in a darkened cockpit.

The circuit breakers for the driving lamps are possibly the most important breakers in the entire system. If the lights 'pop' a breaker then you may be plunged into

As the lighting requirements get higher the demands placed on the alternator and loom increase. (PIAA UK)

Another road-rally innovation; this navigation lamp is actually a reversing lamp mounted on the sun-visor. (Clive Chapman)

darkness, which could very quickly end in disaster. Familiarise yourself and your co-driver with the position of these CBs and make sure that they are placed in a position that is easily accessible by both occupants. Whoever makes the lunge to the popped CB first is likely to be the hero of the hour!

While we are discussing the other occupant of the rally car let us think about their requirements. A stalk light is a fairly traditional way of casting light upon the map; however it is far from ideal. The flexible stalk they are mounted on can be displaced by a heavy landing or aggressive manoeuvre, and the pattern of light generated by these devices is not very regular, meaning the light can be scattered in a manner which could prove off-putting to the driver. For this reason a second type of map light is in use, known due to its peculiar shape as a Potti, or Poti. The Poti is a form of fixed-focus magnifying glass which is placed directly upon the map. The construction is such that the lens is held away from the map by the housing at just the right distance to create a perfect focus. Integral to the Poti is a lighting system which is not visible to the driver, minimising distraction and glare.

The first of these magnifiers was a variation of a type available to the RAF aircrew during the war, and was pioneered by a navigator called Don Barrow. Right from their conception these map lights have been very popular with navigators, and the Don Barrow range of magnifiers specifically (he has always detested the name 'Poti') are very common. This is mainly due to their high-quality construction and ease of use, despite their price being a little higher than more basic magnifiers, due to the use of crystal glass lenses. Another type of lamp useful to our navigator is known as the cage lamp, which clamps directly to the roll cage. This can be switched on to provide spot illumination, and can provide a useful back-up in the event of a navigator's lamp failure.

Finally, a larger lamp mounted around the sun visor area will provide excellent lighting for plotting and such. For those on a budget an old reversing light or small camping fluorescent tube is ideal for this purpose. It is important that these lighting systems take different feeds; if all the lighting goes through one form of circuit protection then the navigator will have nothing to fall back on in the event of a circuit failure. Remember that the lighting should be white out of preference; using a coloured lamp will mean that markings on the map the same colour as the bulb will become invisible.

The latest and most impressive development in automotive lighting systems is undoubtedly the Xenon-based high intensity discharge system. Whilst this system is not exactly new (Osram introduced the first of the breed in 1951 for use in film projectors), it is only recently that the associated ballast units have been made compact and efficient enough to use in the automotive industry. The BMW 7 series of 1991 was the first production car to be fitted with HID technology, and the system has been refined and improved by various manufacturers to the point where today, it is possible to upgrade most vehicles to HID lighting. However, just fitting a HID lighting unit in a reflector designed to take a filament lamp rarely produces the correct light output, and can often result in poor beam dispersion and headlamp dipping. In a normal filament lamp a thin wire has current passed through it, and because of the narrowness of the wire a resistance is encountered. This resistance causes the generation of heat, which causes the filament to glow to the extent that light is emitted.

In an HID system an electric arc is set up similar to that generated when arc welding. In a filament lamp the light generated comes from a straight emitter; the filament stretched between two metal posts. This means that normal reflectors are designed to take the light produced by this straight filament and project it on to the road. As its name suggests, the electric arc is bowed, and produces a very different light pattern within the headlamp. Therefore, a headlamp designed to project filament lamp light is inefficient when a HID unit is fitted with no further modification. To get effective results the HID reflector needs to have been designed for this purpose, as the lamp manufacturers will tell you, if asked.

One of the main advantages of HID lighting is its greater efficiency. A HID lighting unit is over 80 per cent more efficient than a similar light output filament lamp, largely due to the fact that energy is not wasted in heat as it is in a filament lamp. For this reason alone, many people upgrade to HID as it is an excellent idea bearing in mind that not only do you get improved light output, but more horsepower is liberated from the engine as the drain upon the alternator is greatly reduced. If you are going to make such a conversion ensure that you carry out the task properly to avoid being left with more efficient, but less effective lighting. The only way to get proper light dispersion is to use reflectors suited for the purpose. Remember that you will also have to find a home for the ballast units, which require mounting firmly, and may also need adequate ventilation to prevent overheating.

To justify the expense of an HID system you may wish to consider the vastly superior life of the bulbs. Normal headlights in a road car are reckoned to have a lifespan of a few hundred hours, while HID lamps have a lifespan of approximately 2,000 hours. The one thing that tends to shorten the lifespan of a filament lamp is vibration. The filament itself is a very fragile wire, capable of being snapped or damaged far more easily than the glass envelope that surrounds it. The HID system does not use a filament as it produces an electric arc and therefore the bulbs themselves are relatively sturdy when compared with their filament lamp counterparts.

Fitting additional lighting normally requires the use of relays and extra wiring to operate the increased loading that high-powered lamps will place upon the system. It could be asked why we should need relays as we already have a headlamp system that can surely take the load of a few extra lamps? As we have said before, manufacturers will not spend more on building a vehicle than is necessary so the

An example of some of the compact yet powerful lighting systems available to the motorsport competitor. (PIAA UK)

wiring used for the headlamps will be of exactly the correct rating to carry the current used by standard bulbs. If they had used heavier gauge wire then the cost of manufacture would have been more, thereby cutting into their profit margin.

The headlamp switch is another example of these 'savings' in action; the terminals will not be heavy enough to take the load of more lamps, but will be fine to drive a relay connected in parallel with the main-beam bulbs. Having a relay operating the lamps also means we can keep the wiring short, cutting down the losses we would get from running long cables from the front of the car to the dashboard. By putting our on/off switch on the dash with a feed taken from the main beam switch we can interrupt the signal that would otherwise tell the relay to latch on. This means we could prevent the extra lighting from operating where its use is prohibited or would cause problems for other motorists. There is a pretty good chance that the lighting we have fitted will use considerably more current than the standard set-up; if this is the case, then we need to ensure that our alternator is capable of providing the power required. If not, then a unit with a higher current output will have to be sourced.

We should not forget about the mechanics of fitting extra lighting. With most front-engined competition vehicles a great deal of effort is put in to moving weight to the rear of the car from the front to improve the weight distribution. When we affix spot light assemblies to the front of the nose of our vehicle we are putting a chunk of weight in just the place from which we have been trying to remove it. For this reason we need to consider the use of lighter materials when manufacturing light pods and brackets, while keeping in mind the requirement for durability.

Sometimes auxiliary driving lamps suffer from poor earthing. This is where the lamp is expected to return the current from the bulb to the bodywork of the car, but has to fight through corrosion, paint and dirt to get there. If you are having problems along these lines then you could consider fitting an extra earth strap to each light unit. This strap does not have to be as thick as this we use on the engine, but instead, only needs to be the same diameter as the cable supplying the unit. Its entire purpose is to provide an easy route for the current between the bodywork and the lamp unit, increasing its reliability. When you come to run the wiring along the bumper consider a quick-connect connector to allow you to remove the light pod or units when they are not being used. Some might view this as an extravagance, but this is the ideal place to use a System 25-style connector, as discussed in Chapter 2.

The requirements for a connector in this situation are good resistance to water and dirt ingress, the ability to seal it with a blanking plug when nothing is connected, and the ability to flow fairly high current without complaint. This means that disconnecting the driving lights electrically becomes the quickest part of the job. Attaching lamp pods is an ideal application for a type of fastener called the Dzus. These fasteners are often used for holding lightweight body panels on to the vehicle as they are able to be removed rapidly. These fasteners require a quarter turn to lock or unlock, and provide a firm and positive physical connection once in place. Dzus fasteners are used a great deal on aircraft, as they make maintenance easier yet ensure the panels they are attached to will not come undone in flight. It could also be worth making a cradle for the lamp pod to sit in when it is not in use as these are expensive bits of kit and could be damaged by careless handling.

No matter how efficient your lighting, no matter how powerful the bulbs or expensive your HID system, they are all going to give the same dull light output when the lenses are covered in a thick coating of mud. Those involved in road rallies are constantly battling the mud that coats their lighting, but sadly, there are few solutions. The first is to try to prevent the mud from reaching the lamps in the first place. This

Rain lights are perfectly placed to collect all the dirt and detritus the track can throw at them!

can be achieved by mounting rubber sheeting or similar on the bumper in a manner that allows it to catch most of the mud sprayed up before it reaches the headlamps. What this does for aerodynamics is best glossed over! Another possibility is mounting washer jets on the headlamps, if not already fitted. Using a dedicated fairly high powered pump, preferably running from a separate reservoir, will give a large quantity of washer fluid at a high enough pressure to make a good attempt at cleaning the lenses. If using a powerful pump remember to make sure all the pipe connections are secure, as they are much more likely to pop off through brute force.

Of course, the one thing you have to ensure is that any modifications you make are within the rules of the event being entered. This does not just go for the rules of the rally; checking you don't fall foul of the law is important if you wish to keep a clean licence. There are very strict regulations laid down for the positioning of lighting on a car and your local MoT station is most likely to be able to provide up-to-date information, or failing that, a friendly traffic officer at your local police station may be able to help. The boy racers have recently fallen in love with blue headlamp bulbs; nice looking they may be, but it is up to the whim of the police officer involved as to whether using them is an offence or not, as to show any blue lamp on a vehicle other than the emergency services is of course illegal. HID lighting has proven to be a bit of a grey area due to the distinctly blue hue the lights give off, but due to the fact that some luxury cars are fitted with this equipment as standard it is unlikely you will be penalised for using such equipment, assuming you are using it in a legal manner. Some road rallies have recently started to ban HID lighting as marshals had complained that 'in future I'll have to bring a welding mask!', so make sure you check with the organisers that whichever system you are using is acceptable for the event in which you are competing.

Chapter 9

Instrumentation, switchgear and engine health monitoring

A GREAT DEAL of time, effort and expense goes into the construction of a race engine. No matter what the state of tune, from a standard Ford Zetec to a Cosworth DFV, it is far cheaper to monitor the health of the engine in use than pick up the pieces after an unmonitored catastrophic failure. Comprehensive instrumentation allows problems (or potential problems) to be picked up early, allowing the driver to adjust his driving style, or take an early bath. However, it is important to strike a balance between comprehensive driver feedback and information overload. The driver has no interest in how great a vacuum is contained within the inlet manifold while tickling 200mph down the Mulsanne Straight. However, it's quite nice to be made aware that the engine may be about to seize solid due to a sudden drop in oil pressure; locked rear wheels mid corner are not a great help to your racing line…

What follows is a basic guide to instrumentation available. There are more instruments on the market, and their absence from this list is not any reflection on their importance. However, those included here are a cross-section of what is obtainable while the applicability of each item is entirely down to you.

Basic instrumentation

Tachometer
The tachometer (or 'rev counter') is one of the most important gauges the driver can use. It tends to be the largest and most centrally positioned instrument. Usually driven from the low tension side of the ignition coil or an output from the engine management, the tachometer gives the engine speed to the driver in a rapidly responding analogue readout. The more expensive tachometers use a stepper motor for accuracy. This is a type of motor which gives a very precise output, and is less likely to be affected by accelerative forces and bumps.

Available in many different rpm ranges, it is important that you pick your tachometer carefully. If your engine has a maximum usable speed of 6,000rpm, a rev counter with a maximum needle deflection marked up to 12,000rpm will lack the visual clarity of one with a more suitable scale. Another important consideration is engine type. As most tachometers count the pulses fed to them by the coil or ECU, the number of pulses supplied will vary, depending on the number of cylinders. A wasted spark system is different again, using two coils for four cylinders, each firing twice per cylinder per cycle. Depending on the design, it may be possible to tap one coil of the wasted spark system, as the number of sparks one of the pair of coils emits should be the same as a single-coil system.

Professional tachometers offer a much greater degree of accuracy than those fitted by the vehicle manufacturer at production. (Stack Ltd)

Simplicity in the cockpit means a reduction in the driver workload. In this case, an 'idiot light' and a tacho keep distractions to a minimum. (Paul Martin)

Despite the tacho being partially obscured by the wheel, the important part of the rev-range is in full view of the driver. Note the recess for the shift light. (Paul Martin)

In this Hillman Imp a large side lamp has been used as an 'idiot light' to grab the driver's attention in the event of a drop in oil pressure. (Wren Classics)

Oil pressure gauge

Often combined with a bright warning lamp and sometimes referred to as an 'idiot light', the oil pressure gauge allows monitoring of the lubricant pressure in the engine. A drop in this pressure noticed early can prevent terminal damage to the engine. Oil pressure gauges come in two types: mechanical and electric. The mechanical types rely on a pipe connected to the engine, whereas the electric types use a pressure sensing sender unit. Whilst the mechanical types are faster to react than the electric type, they tend to need more effort to fit, and the pipe line connecting them to the oil system can also be a weak point. Adding any extra tubing to a pressurised system is not without its risks. The safety aspect of keeping hot fluids out of the driver's compartment is not to be ignored either.

Water temperature gauge

Only applicable to water-cooled engines of course, water temperature gauges give valuable information about how well the engine is performing. For example, an engine pumping out more heat than usual could be suffering from ignition timing problems, or a malfunctioning cooling system, among other things. During the early testing stages of a new competition vehicle, the water temperature gauge will allow us to assess the suitability of the car's cooling arrangement, such as the capability of the radiator.

The primary use of a water temperature gauge is during racing, monitoring this gauge allows the driver to keep a close eye on the health of the cooling system. Available in electric and mechanical (or capillary) types, the electric type is considerably more common. It may be of interest to note that as standard, modern production cars run relatively high temperatures to ensure the catalytic converter runs closest to its optimum operating temperature. As more power is produced at lower engine temperatures, racing engines, which are pushed a great deal more than their production counterparts, are ideally run at lower temperatures.

Oil temperature gauge

At first, the importance of oil temperature could be misjudged. As we already have a water temperature gauge for our competition car, why should we bother monitoring the oil temperature as well? As oil heats up its viscosity drops, reducing the film strength between bearing surfaces. Multigrade oils are designed to combat this, but even these have an optimum running temperature. Turbocharged cars use the oil contained in the sump for cooling and lubricating the bearing at the centre of the turbo. If the oil gets too hot then heat cannot be drawn away from the turbocharger as effectively, possibly leading to premature failure of the bearing. When heated above a certain temperature, oil breaks down irreversibly, losing some of its lubricating characteristics.

If an oil cooler is fitted without an oil-stat (a thermostat that prevents the oil being sent to the oil cooler until it is warm enough to require cooling) then the oil can run too cold, never reaching its optimum operating temperature. Therefore it becomes obvious that oil temperature is quite critical in the healthy running of a performance engine. Usually an oil temperature gauge is of similar construction to a water temperature gauge. When testing, an oil temperature gauge allows the driver to judge when the oil is at a useful operating temperature, and can therefore be driven as it would be during a race. If a problem occurs with the bottom end of the engine, increased friction causes an increase in lubricant temperature.

Stock car racers in America actually use the oil temperature gauge as an aid to aerodynamics. This is not as strange as might first appear; the oil temperature gauge is monitored while individually covering the cooling holes on the front of the car. The

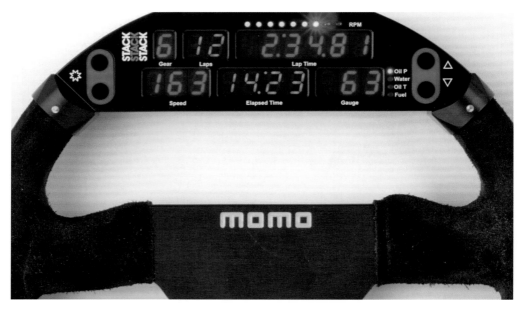

In a single-seater where space is at a premium, steering wheel-mounted instrumentation such as this can be advantageous. (Stack Ltd)

car is tested, and the oil temperature monitored and as many holes are covered as is possible without causing an increase in the coolant temperature. As these holes cause drag and are aerodynamically unclean, the fewer holes required to keep the engine cool the better.

Fuel pressure gauge

Monitoring fuel pressure could be deemed slightly less important than many of the other parameters available to the driver. However, as a tool for diagnosis it could provide some rapid answers when the car coasts into the pit lane mid-race. To over simplify, when an engine fails to run, it is usually due to one of two things: fuel problems or ignition faults. By giving some information on one of these systems diagnosis can be started before the car has even chugged to a halt. A drop in fuel pressure, caused by blocked fuel lines or a faulty fuel pump for example, will show up on the gauge. However, as the use of the information gathered from this gauge could be considered rather specialised, it is probably best not to give this instrument pride of place over the tachometer in your dashboard layout. If space and weight considerations allow it however, it could be a useful addition.

Ammeter

The ammeter gives accurate information on how much current is being used by the vehicle systems. A centre-biased needle on a scale extending to a negative and a positive quantity each side (usually –30 to +30, or –60 to +60 amps), the ammeter requires all the current to be measured to be sent through it. This means that with the exception of the starter motor, all the electrics used by the vehicle must be wired through the ammeter in series. This does necessitate some rather heavy duty cables running directly behind the dashboard, and a failure of the ammeter (however rare an event this may be) would result in a total loss of the vehicle's electrical system.

This Mk2 Escort hill-climb car has a simple and inexpensive dash layout, which is more than adequate for its racing. (Paul Martin)

In defence of the humble ammeter for monitoring the state of the charging system there is no finer method. Giving accurate information on the rate of charge (or discharge) of the battery tells us how much work the alternator is doing. If during use of fairly heavy load electrical devices (such as heaters) the ammeter shows a discharge, then this is a good indication that the alternator is not up to the task of powering all the systems, or is faulty. However, I believe that an ammeter is not an important requirement for a competition car, and I am not alone. Stewart Warner no longer sells a competition-grade ammeter, as its uses are so limited in this age of ultra-efficient compact alternators and low-current draw components, that demand does not warrant its production.

Voltmeter
A lot simpler to fit when compared with an ammeter, a voltmeter provides similar information. When the engine is not running, and therefore the alternator is not charging the battery, a voltmeter tells us the voltage held by the battery at that time. This gives us a good indication of the state of charge of the battery, and therefore its suitability for use. When the starting system comes online the voltage increases, which is reflected in the reading on the gauge. This allows us to verify the health of the charging system.

A voltmeter can be fitted anywhere there is a positive feed, and does not need to be fitted in series as the ammeter does. However, it should be noted that a voltmeter also measures the voltage drop over the cables that supply it. To clarify, if a voltmeter is fitted far away from the battery, the resistance of the cables that supply it will drop the voltage received by the gauge, which will in turn result in a lower reading. Admittedly, this voltage drop may be small, but in the interests of accuracy the voltmeter should ideally be placed as close to the battery and charging system as is possible. Due to their simplicity and versatility in use, I prefer to use a voltmeter in a competition car over an ammeter.

Fuel gauge

A fuel gauge simply informs the driver of the quantity of fuel he is carrying. However, standard automotive fuel gauges tend to be misleading. It is common belief that some manufacturers use fuel gauges that operate more slowly at the top end of their scale, as it is within the first 200–300 miles that new owners will be getting their first impressions of the car, including its fuel economy. As the fuel level drops, the needle increases in its speed of movement with relation to the fuel being used. This psychological trickery is the reason that most production car fuel gauges tend to stay on full for a long time after refuelling, despite many miles being covered. This gives the impression that the vehicle has an excellent fuel range…

Most racing cars will be fitted with racing fuel cells, which either have no form of quantative measurement, a sight glass, or an inbuilt sender unit to provide an output to a gauge. In each of these cases the standard manufacturer's fuel gauge is not required, and can be removed. This frees up dashboard space for more important instruments. The inconvenience when this removal takes place in a road car is one of the hardships that a road/race car owner must endure! If the facility is available however, it is prudent to include it, if only to avoid potentially embarrassing 'why won't it start?' moments!

Speedometer

Unless the regulations specifically request a speedometer is fitted, or the car is required to pass an MoT test, this is possibly the least important gauge a competition car can have. Rarely does a driver have a chance to check his speed while driving at ten-tenths, although if striving for improvement of lap times or comparing modifications carried out in testing, a speedometer may be of some small use. For the most part, competition cars dispense with this instrument. If there is a requirement for road use, then the speedometer should be as small and unobtrusive as possible. Whilst the importance of obeying road traffic laws cannot be overemphasised, driving is less stressful on the road, and the siting of gauges of lesser importance is not quite as significant a problem. However, having an instrument such as the tachometer within easy view is very important when the eyes are focused on the track ahead.

Boost gauge

A boost gauge is only a requirement on a vehicle with forced induction. This allows you to see exactly how much assisted induction is taking place. When building an engine with forced induction the design takes into account the pressure that you intend to run, and this gauge allows the pressure to be monitored and set. Once set it gives information on the health of the turbo/supercharger, showing under-pressurisation due to compressor/turbine failure, or over-pressurisation due to wastegate actuator failure for example.

Transmission/axle temperature gauges

There are very few vehicles that require in-depth monitoring of transmission and axle temperatures. One notable exception to this was the TVR Speed 12 built to race the British GT series. During the original design process the exhausts were routed down the centre of the car, resulting in an enlarged transmission tunnel and a centre exit exhaust system. However, it was soon discovered that the oil cooler required for the differential was larger than that required for the engine! If it is believed that transmission/axle temperature will be an issue then it is possible to carefully tap the casing of these, or if they are supplied by an oil pump, an in-line transducer can be fitted. However, the worth of this instrumentation on most racing vehicles is debatable.

The greater the driver feedback the quicker a fault can be diagnosed under pressure.
(Simon Crosse)

Exhaust gas temperature (EGT)
There was a time when exhaust gas temperature gauges were the sole reserve of aircraft. However in this time of highly stressed turbocharged cars, the EGT is becoming a more and more common addition. Used in many World Rally Cars, this gauge gives feedback on the health of the turbocharger and the accuracy of the engine management, and allows the driver to assess when it is safe to switch off the engine (as switching the engine off when the EGT is high can lead to premature turbocharger failure).

EGT gauges use a thermocouple to pick up its temperature reading. In its simplest form a thermocouple is a junction of two wires made from different metals. When heat is applied to this junction it produces a small voltage directly proportional to the heat applied. If we calibrate a gauge to this voltage we can measure some very high temperatures, far in excess of that we could measure with a normal temperature sender. An EGT set-up usually consists of a gauge, a thermocouple and a control unit. The control unit is a small box that interprets the signals sent from the thermocouples and provides a drive for the gauge. The thermocouple is normally mounted in the exhaust manifold, as placing it after the turbocharger would increase response time and reduce accuracy.

Warning lights
It used to be common practice amongst rally teams to fit a large amber light, such as an indicator side repeater, to the dashboard of the rally car, right in the driver's line of sight. This provides a stark visual warning in the event of oil pressure loss, which if not caught in time would have catastrophic consequences for the engine. Some people also use a large lamp for the ignition lamp, although of course a generator failure, whilst probably debilitating, should not destroy your engine. The oil pressure switch is sometimes wired through a relay; in the 'on' position (oil pressure high) it

provides a live feed to the ignition and fuel pumps, and in the 'off' position (oil pressure low) it kills the feed to the ignition and fuel pumps and illuminates the warning light. This system is a great idea, but suffers from two shortcomings. The first is the requirement for a bypass switch to allow the engine to be started, which needs to be depressed until the oil pressure is high enough to operate the relay and sustain itself. The second is that any brief interruptions in the oil supply, such as an oil surge due to poor sump baffling, will cause the engine to die when there is no real risk to it. It is during the assessment of such devices that the importance of proper and exhaustive testing of your competition car becomes apparent!

Other lights available for less important warnings are diverse, and are available in many shapes, sizes, colours and abilities. As LEDs become cheaper with every passing day, available in more colours and capable of more things than ever before, the competition car dashboard is less likely to be dominated by filaments as time goes on. Filaments (otherwise known rather archaically as bulbs) have served their time now; prone to failure in harsh conditions, drawing more current than their more reliable semiconductor cousins, and are bulkier, and more fragile. Conversely, LEDs are very unlikely to fail (assuming they are wired correctly, in the correct polarity and with a ballast resistor), very light on their current demands, compact and sturdy, being constructed of a very hard resin.

Some LEDs incorporate microprocessors which allow them to blink when supplied with power, while others will illuminate one colour when current is applied in one

Despite already boasting excellent instrumentation, the operators of this Ferrari 360 Challenge have mounted an extra shift light directly in the driver's line of sight. Notice the alcantara dash covering to reduce reflection on the inside of the screen. (Wren Classics)

Some instruments have the ability to show more than just the information they are primarily intended to deliver. (Stack Ltd)

direction, and illuminate a totally different colour when polarity is reversed. Shift lights are usually LEDs, due to their bright and focused illumination. Car manufacturers are starting to use LEDs as brake lights on their top-end vehicles. It is my belief that an LED brake lamp is safer than a filament unit, due partially to its reliability, but mainly because the reaction time of an LED is appreciably faster than a filament. This may seem to be of little importance, but the instant illumination afforded by an LED is a lot more noticeable than the slightly lethargic reaction of a filament. If that means I am less likely to receive a rear end shunt, then I am all in favour of this incoming trend!

Aircraft operate a system called the 'dark cockpit' technique; during normal operation with all systems operating within their normal parameters, no lights are illuminated in the cockpit. This means that if a warning lamp is illuminated it will be immediately noticed, and in normal use there are an absolute minimum of distractions to the driver.

Integrated instrument systems

When dashboard space is paramount, or light weight is an overriding priority, the ability to combine a multitude of instruments into one convenient readout is a definite bonus. With an intelligent display system, only anomalies are highlighted, and the display can be modified to show the parameters of direct interest to the driver. Another possibility is the integration of the system with a lap timing device, displaying the lap time briefly as the trackside sensor is passed, before reverting to the previous display. One of the systems commercially available is the Stack ST8100 Display. This set-up consists of a triangular pod incorporating an accurate tachometer and an LCD display capable of showing a number of different parameters. In its most basic form the unit is capable of displaying oil pressure and temperature, water temperature, fuel pressure and battery voltage, with optional upgrade packs allowing the fitment of wheel speed and lap time sensors to provide information for additional displays.

The equipment can also be upgraded to incorporate accelerometer inputs for use with the data logging system. All the standard parameters can be set to flag up a warning should some preset thresholds be exceeded, such as a coolant overheat or a drop in oil pressure. Up to four parameters can be displayed simultaneously, but anything that needs to be brought to the attention of the driver (such as a loss of oil pressure) takes precedence over the parameters being displayed at the time, and therefore replaces it on the display. The system also stores any peak values for assessment at a later date which allows teams without access to data logging software to retrieve the highest values displayed by the device. Integrated into the face of the unit near the tachometer is the shift light, programmable to advise the driver that the optimum gear change point has been reached.

When used in conjunction with a lap timing beacon the system is capable of displaying the lap times to the driver, while an additional logging system will record the timing data (along with the other parameters). For vehicles which are required to pass an MoT test, the Stack system is also available with an odometer, speedometer, trip meter and fuel gauge, making the system a viable possibility for a vehicle used on a daily basis.

The advantages of replacing six or seven instruments with a single pod cannot be ignored, and while the cost of this system is higher than using individual gauges, the weight saving and technological leap forward this system gives is certainly a factor worth considering when constructing a competition vehicle.

Mounting your instruments

When positioning instruments it is worth considering the orientation of the gauge. In a bank of instruments, it is a practice often seen in aviation to mount the gauge so that the needle is vertical when in its normal operating range. This means that when the pilot/driver glances at his instrumentation it is immediately apparent when a reading is outside of the required envelope. Of course, this does reduce the readability of the numbers and legend written on the gauge, which will usually require remarking with the designation of the instrument. When marking instruments it is useful to invest in some form of label making device; these vary in price but perform basically the same task. These handy little units usually produce labels of around 10–20mm in width and to whatever length you require. They produce a self-adhesive, clear, and easy-to-read label which tends to be very durable in my experience. If you require a more 'retro' look to your vehicle dashboard, such as a reproduction of a classic competition car, then the older style of Dymo label making machine frequently appears on sale in places such as eBay. However, the adhesive qualities of such labels are probably past their best by now.

Instrument selection

When selecting a gauge for your cockpit it is vital that the clarity of the markings is considered. In general the larger the sweep of a gauge's needle, the greater the accuracy of the readout. For optimum accuracy a gauge of 270° sweep is ideal. However, for the less important systems a reduced sweep (as is found on most electric gauges) is sufficient. It should be stated that it is good practice to stick to one form of gauge; if a 270° gauge is to be used then the preference is that this should be used for as many instruments as possible. It is far easier to notice an aberrant temperature or pressure when all of the gauges operate in a similar manner. Various diameters can be purchased, and the size of the gauge in the cockpit should reflect its importance to the driver.

Choosing an instrument to monitor a specific parameter requires a little research into the requirements you have of the set-up. When selecting a temperature gauge for

The better specification dashboard systems can be configured to display other information, such as the lap time data shown here.

Sometimes more expensive systems can be emulated with a little ingenuity and a few cable-ties!

example, it is vital that the correct temperature range is selected. If you purchase a gauge which does not go up to the required values, the needle will reach a stage known as *full scale deflection*. This is where the indicating needle is required to display a value beyond the design parameters of the instrument and it therefore goes off of the scale. Conversely, if the temperature you wish to measure is much lower than the capabilities of the instrument, the gauge may be inaccurate. Consider an EGT gauge misused to display water temperature; an average EGT gauge is capable of displaying temperatures of up to 900°C, nine times the point at which water boils at normal atmospheric pressure. Therefore, in theory, only the first 11 per cent of the gauge would actually be used. If the gauge had a sweep of 88°, only the first 8° of sweep would be usable (this is assuming that the EGT even goes down to a figure that low). Of course, this is an extreme example, but it does neatly illustrate the importance of selecting your scale astutely.

Most instruments require a 12V supply, if you are not confident that the electrical system is capable of providing a stable output then a voltage stabiliser should be considered. As the name suggests, this is a device which takes the incoming voltage and makes it less likely to fluctuate, providing more accurate instrument readings. Obviously you should not run your voltmeter through this unit! Most high-quality instruments are quite tolerant of minor voltage changes, and normally there is little requirement for such a device. On older cars a voltage regulator was fitted that operated very slowly, often giving one pulse of current every second. The reason this did not produce fluctuations in the reading is down to the design of the instruments. Each gauge was designed to have a very slow reaction time, often with some form of damping integral to the design. This allowed unimportant changes in the signals from the sender units to be disregarded, such as fluctuations from the fuel tank sender as the fuel moves around the tank during cornering. Due to the sluggish operation of these gauges they are seldom up to the task of feeding back information at the speed and accuracy that is required by a competition driver, and the regulators are of no use with modern gauges due to their slow and imprecise operation. Therefore, a more modern semiconductor system is better suited to the task. As stated previously, there is little requirement for this device on a modern competition car, as modern instruments are much more stable and tolerant of minute variations in voltage.

If your vehicle is never likely to be used at night then instrument illumination is probably of little importance to you, but it pays to think in the long term. By wiring in the illumination systems of your instruments you are effectively 'future-proofing' your competition car. If you decide to change racing series, or the competition you currently compete in decides to incorporate a night or late evening event, suddenly the dashboard has to come out to loom in a system of illumination. Using instruments from the same manufacturer makes it easier to maintain some form of conformity with the internal lighting and variations of lighting techniques across the dashboard can be disconcerting, making it harder to read the gauges. If some form of dimmer system is intended, instruments lit using different filaments or techniques will result in uneven dimming across the dashboard. If such a system is required, then it is a simple matter of wiring the instrument lighting in series with a variable resistor. This method could be frowned upon due to it being rather wasteful (a semiconductor-based dimming circuit would draw less current), but the advantages derived from the simplicity of construction far outweighs the disadvantages of a very slightly higher current consumption.

Although the colour of an instrument's face may seem a trifling matter, the driver may find certain colour combinations are easier to read than others, especially in times of high driver workload. The best way of finding out which is best for you is to print out a copy of the instrument faces in the colours that are available and which should be easy to find on the manufacturers' websites. Alternatively, simply cutting out the images you require from their brochure will have much the same effect. Once you have a mock up of these instruments it is pretty easy to decide which unit shows a greater clarity in use. Needless to say, a paper cut-out does not have the luxury of backlighting!

Often there are a number of options when selecting an instrument bezel with chrome and matt black finishes being just two of the main options on offer. It is important to consider glare and reflection in the cockpit and whilst it is not likely that the reflection from a highly polished chrome bezel will blind the driver, it may briefly distract him, or could even appear momentarily to be a warning lamp coming on. This could divert the driver's attention at a crucial moment, so I prefer to use as many non-reflective materials in my vehicle dash set-up as is reasonably possible. Painting the dashboard with a matt black paint provides a professional looking finish, with a minimum of reflectivity.

The needle of an instrument should strike a fine balance between large width (for high visibility) and narrow width (for greater accuracy). There is a plethora of instruments on the market, and as with every other variable discussed here, it really is personal preference as to which you decide is most suited to the task in hand.

A quick note on the fitting of sender units; if a sealant is used (such as PTFE tape) you may discover that your reading is inaccurate, or even non-existent. This is because the senders use a connection to earth through the engine block, and utilising a sealant material can insulate the sender, interrupting the circuit.

Digital instrumentation

Digital instruments are becoming more and more commonplace, especially in systems that have previously not been very easy to monitor. SPA Design market a range of instruments with a digital readout that fit in the same diameter hole that normally accommodates an analogue gauge. Whilst more expensive than their analogue counterparts, the digital versions have numerous advantages, such as greater accuracy, in-built warning lamps, and often an ability to change the units of measurement they display (such as imperial to metric). Previously it has been very difficult to verify exactly how much bias has been applied to a braking system's front/rear split. SPA now manufacture a brake bias gauge capable of giving an accurate readout to the driver. They are capable of providing either a pressure reading or a percentage split reading, and are designed to be visually intuitive in use. Of course, how much use this system will be depends entirely on the type of motorsport being competed in. One of the more useful designs provided by SPA is the combined boost and EGT gauge, providing two very important figures for those running a turbocharger in an easy-to-read compact format.

Using a digital readout removes a phenomenon known as 'parallax error'. When looking at an analogue instrument reading 35psi, moving your line of vision to the left of the gauge will produce an apparent reading of more than 35psi, despite the fact that the needle has not moved. Moving your line of vision to the right will make the gauge appear to have a lower reading (assuming the needle is pivoted from the bottom and the scale has a marking starting with zero on the left-hand side). The greater the distance between the needle and the scale, the greater this problem becomes. Usually, the issue is not too important as the instruments are mounted to face the driver. However, as dashboard space becomes tighter, the instruments will become mounted further and further away, especially those which do not require constant assessment. Digital gauges remove this problem, as the figures required are displayed in an easy-to-read numerical format. On the other hand, it is harder to detect a trend on a digital instrument; a temperature which is slowly creeping up may be easier to notice on an analogue instrument for instance. The choice of gauge is most likely to be down to budget and driver preference.

Ergonomics

If designing a cockpit layout from scratch then it is often a good idea to 'mock-up' the predicted layout of instrumentation. After spending hours building a dashboard it can be rather disheartening to find that a vital instrument is obscured by the steering wheel. If you can briefly ignore the laughter of your friends, making cardboard cut-outs of the instruments you intend to use and Blu-tacking them to your dashboard can provide a useful tool for designing an ergonomically efficient arrangement. Consider the placement of the hands when holding the wheel in a natural position; try to emulate your normal driving position as much as is possible. From this position the tacho and oil pressure (or similarly important warning lights) should fall easily within view, requiring minimal movement of the head and eyes to monitor them. It is possible to use a very bright LED for the shift lamp; by mounting the LED in such a manner that it reflects off of the inside surface of the windscreen directly within the driver's field of view a head-up display arrangement can be achieved. However, this effect could be compromised in bright sunlight, so a second LED in a more conventional position is advised.

The author's current competition vehicle has the shift lamp mounted within the tachometer; a very simple modification which means that the eyes do not have to move too far from the important instruments in use. Naturally, great care should be

An obscured instrument may as well not be there at all.

This instrumentation system displays a great deal of information to the driver while taking up a minimum of dashboard space. (Stack Ltd)

taken when dismantling instruments as it is all too easy to dislodge or disturb something that could have a great effect on the accuracy of the gauge. This is a procedure that could conceivably be carried out on an oil pressure gauge for example when integrating the oil pressure warning lamp in to the face. Again, this requires the dismantling of the instrument which may cause issues with accuracy and possibly invalidate the warranty. As with most modifications of this type it is best to proceed with great caution and plenty of prudence!

When your cardboard instrument cluster has reached its final evolution, with every instrument in a position that is easy to read, it is time to start thinking about the construction of the dash. If the switchgear has yet to be placed it is prudent to do this first; remember that the more important the switch, the easier the accessibility should be. Don't forget to ensure that accidental operation is a risk to be kept to a minimum. Switch guards are available to prevent a flailing hand from operating something unintentionally, although it is usually far easier to place the switch in a position where the risk is minimised in the first place.

Consider the movements you will have to carry out to enter and exit the vehicle. The stalk can easily be kicked off of a switch while playing roll cage limbo! It makes sense to group certain instruments together; oil and water temperature make neat partners, as do oil pressure and oil temp. If both a voltmeter and ammeter are used, pairing these is sensible. Divide the instrument cluster into sections; one group of gauges could cover engine health, the next cover the electrical system, another could cover capacities. Switchgear should be grouped in a similar manner as this allows rapid driver familiarisation within his environment. If it is possible to automate a system then this could be an advantage, as this reduces the clutter of switches in the

OVERLEAF *This Chevron has a clear dashboard layout with well marked switchgear. Note the large warning lights for improved visibility in the heat of racing.* (Wren Classics)

driver's compartment. However, when competition car systems are automated most drivers prefer some form of override, thus requiring a switch, so nothing is gained. More on system automation is covered in Chapter 10.

Switchgear

Manufacturers of production cars have deviated away from toggle type switches as they usually project into the passenger compartment in a manner that could cause injury in the event of an accident. One exception to this is BMW with the Mini where, by shrouding each switch with a semi-elliptical guard, the risk to occupants in a collision has been minimised. I prefer to use toggle switches due to their visual clarity and at a glance I can tell if they are engaged without requiring power to illuminate a warning lamp. They are available in both plastic and metal varieties and obviously the metal ones are more resistant to breakage. This might not be the advantage it may first appear as if it is your kneecap that hits the switch at speed it may be preferable that the switch is the weaker of the two colliding objects! For durability however, I have always been biased towards high-quality metal toggle switches.

Switches come in a variety of types. A toggle remains in the position in which it has been left, a momentary switch will return to its previous position when the operating force has been removed. This is best demonstrated by highlighting some possible uses for a toggle and momentary switch. A toggle switch would be ideal for the windscreen wipers, whereas a momentary switch would be best suited to the washers. Some toggle switches have three positions, with the central position being 'off', and the two extremes being two separate 'on' positions. This would be suited to an indicator set-up for example.

Toggle switches are available in four main types:

SPST – single pole single throw; a simple 'on/off' switch.

DPST – double pole single throw; two 'on/off' switches ganged together in one package.

SPDT – single pole double throw; a switch with two positions, both 'on'. When only wired in to one 'throw' of the switch it acts as an SPST.

DPDT – double pole double throw; a switch consisting of two SPDTs ganged together in one package.

The DPDT switches tend to be the same or similarly sized when compared with their SPST counterparts, so if future system expansion is envisaged it makes sense to use just DPDT switches. A DPDT switch has all the characteristics of the other switches, so can be used as an SPST for example, and yet can still be utilised if systems get upgraded.

When mounting your switches, consider fitting them in a manner that means that in normal use all the switchgear will appear to be in the same state; ie all toggles facing down, or all toggles facing up. This means that during use the systems can all be seen to be set to 'race condition', and nothing will be forgotten. If the engine dies on the grid, a quick visual check of the switchgear is easier if the switches all conform to a preset pattern the driver has memorised. If all the switches are facing the same direction, this will confirm that all the equipment required for use has been switched on, and any switchgear used for diagnostics, fuel pump priming or starting purposes has been returned to its normal position.

Clear marking of switches is vital, not only as to what a switch operates, but in which position the switch is on. A lamp for each switch can be an aid to demonstrating that a system is operating, but this has a few disadvantages. The first is that it contravenes the principles of the dark cockpit technique. Secondly, it is extra weight and complication. And thirdly, a lamp illuminated is not necessarily proof that its system is operating. A better technique is a system in which a lamp illuminates if the system is *not* operating as expected.

Consider a fuel pump; a primitive system will have a lamp supplied by the power output from the operating switch. This means that when power is applied to the pump the lamp is illuminated. However a lamp connected to a fuel line pressure switch would mean that the lamp would illuminate whenever there is no pressure in the fuel line; ie a problem with the fuel supply system. This conforms to our dark cockpit ideology, gives an indication that a fault has occurred (and not just a pump fault, it could help indicate a leak or similar component failure) and gives visual verification that the system is operating as required. Of course, a filament failure would make it appear that the system is healthy, which is why warning lamps in aircraft are fitted with a 'push-to-test' facility. When the bezel of the lamp is depressed, current is passed through the filament to verify that it is operating correctly. Obviously, this test should be carried out before each use of the vehicle. As with any filament used, a set of spares is always a useful addition to your tool box (properly protected of course!).

Chapter 10

Safety systems and automation

The dawn of semiconductor systems has made electronic equipment more compact and more reliable with every passing day. A few years ago the thought of using electronically triggered safety equipment was laughable, as where the technology did exist it was temperamental at best. This meant that systems such as plumbed-in fire extinguishers had to be operated with a Bowden cable, which limited the number of places they could be mounted. These days the reliability of semiconductor devices has meant that more and more mechanically triggered components have started to be replaced with their lighter and smaller electronic counterparts. While some more budget-conscious teams still use Bowden cable-operated devices, most have now moved on to electronic types, which can be mounted some distance from the bottle itself. These are often capable of having several trigger buttons at some distance from the control box, and can be easily isolated to prevent accidental discharge. There are certain precautions that have to be taken however.

If we wish to inhibit a mechanically operated extinguisher from discharging accidentally then the best course of action is to place some form of safety pin into the operating linkage. This must be accessible to whomever needs to fit and remove the pin, and it must isolate all operating T-handles and cable pulls. The safety pin needs to be fitted with a prominent warning flag to ensure there is no chance of it being left in place when the extinguisher is required to be in the armed condition, and a strict ritual should be standard practice as part of the pre-race routine to ensure that it is removed before every use of the vehicle.

With an electronic trigger the control box is usually placed in a prominent position within the driver's reach, as it normally contains both the arming switch and a trigger button. These units are usually powered by a self-contained battery to ensure they will still operate if the electrical power is disconnected, so care should still be taken even when there are no other electrical components fitted to the car. When fitting these systems it is prudent to borrow a technique from our closest engineering partners again: aerospace. When routing any cable that is used to fire a pyrotechnic device, whether a flare or a missile, aeroplane manufacturers ensure that the cables that operate these devices are placed at some distance from other looms. This is because any stray EMF generated by the cables could generate a current in the armament cables which could in turn trigger the explosive device. The shielding on the cables used in the fire extinguisher systems should prevent this, and although the results of a fire extinguisher going off at an unexpected time could be dangerous it is certainly less of a risk than an uncommanded detonation of a weapon on a fighter jet!

So the message is, where possible, avoid other looms, but if this is impossible or difficult don't lose too much sleep over it. If you have previously been careful about routing cables to avoid chafing then you should apply this principle even more effectively when routing the trigger wiring. Careful routing of the loom will ensure that nothing can damage it, as if the insulation is broken through to the wiring beneath shorting or cutting the cables within, the extinguisher could fire either when the system is initially armed, or during a race. At best this is going to be an unexpected annoyance, at worst this could be responsible for the driver losing control of the car due to his concentration being disrupted or vision obscured. Halon used to be the fire extinguisher agent of choice, specifically Bromochlorodifluoromethane, usually abbreviated to BCF. It is now no longer in production due to its harmful effects on people and the environment, and the only two extinguishing agents permitted by the MSA for plumbed-in extinguishers are AFFF and Zero 2000. AFFF stands for aqueous film forming foam, and interestingly it consists of the same chemical as used in the production of Teflon, namely perfluorooctanic acid. While less harmful than Halon it is still a bit of an unknown quantity, and coming into contact with AFFF should be avoided. The Zero 2000 system is a trade name used by the Lifeline Company, as their own composition of foam extinguisher gained MSA/FIA homologation in 1999.

When installing a fire extinguisher make sure you obey the manufacturer's instructions on the correct orientation when mounting the unit. These are not guidelines, it's mandatory if you want the extinguisher to operate correctly. Some extinguishers use a weighted flexible pickup tube, meaning it does not matter which

A good plumbed-in fire extinguisher can mean the difference between 'singed' and 'salvageable' and the loss of a lot of expensive equipment. (Terry Lawless)

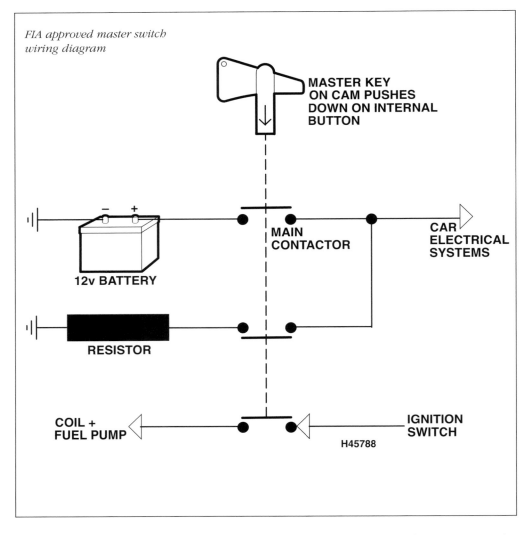

way they are mounted, while one manufacturer utilises a sack containing the extinguishing medium, kept separate from the propellant. This means that when the extinguisher is triggered the entire contents of the sack leaves the nozzle, whilst the propellant remains in the bottle on the other side of the sack. As this system is more efficient (on others, some extinguishing media remains in the bottle and has to be taken into account during the design phase) it can be smaller while maintaining the same quantity of extinguishing media expelled. Interestingly the MSA quote the preferred method of operating the plumbed-in extinguisher as being electrical, with a separate source of electricity for triggering, preferring not to muck around with the mechanically triggered type at all.

If you do decide to use a mechanical type, ensure it uses a one shot 'total discharge' type valve. This means that when the T-handle is pulled the extinguisher discharges and does not stop until it is empty, regardless of the position of the handle. If this type of valve was not fitted the operator would have to keep the handle pulled until the fire was out, which really isn't desirable. Also bear in mind that to check that the extinguisher is at its correct weight (to ensure it hasn't been discharged) it will need to be easily removable. Some extinguishers utilise a quick release coupling to the discharge tubes which makes this job a lot easier, but make sure you replace them properly when you refit the bottle.

As we are removing the mechanisation from the extinguisher system it makes sense for us to look at the battery isolate switch as well. When we examine battery isolators in detail it is rather surprising that a system that is by its very nature electrical relies on mechanical control. One of the most limiting factors of using a mechanical switch to isolate our battery is the requirement to either route the cables to a switch near the driver or use a mechanical extension, such as a Bowden cable, to operate it.

Companies including Armtech have now manufactured a system utilising a chassis-mounted box containing a high-current remote switch that can be positioned anywhere in the car. This allows us to place the switch very near the battery, reducing the length of cable run required. The Armtech system uses two red battery kill buttons, a large one to be placed externally alongside the extinguisher button or T-handle, and another in the cockpit for use by the driver. This smaller switch is complimented by a green power on switch to allow the power to be restored to the car. This places control with the driver, and allows for a much more flexible system than using a simple mechanical switch. However at ten times the price of the basic mechanical switch these improvements do not come cheap, but if only for the increased safety and convenience this is a piece of equipment well worth considering.

The emergency electrical cut-off should be clearly marked and accessible, shown here mounted in an unusual place on this Aston Martin race car. (Wren Classics)

OPPOSITE *In this racing Hillman Imp a T-handle attached to a cable is used to operate the dash mounted electrical cut-off switch.* (Wren Classics)

ABOVE *An FIA approved electrical cut-off switch.* (Grayston Engineering)

It is pretty unusual to discuss the disabling of safety systems, but there are times when devices designed to improve our safety on the road will actually cause us more difficulties on the track. The first example of this is the inertia fuel cut-off switch fitted to modern cars. This is a device which turns off the fuel pump in the event of an accident causing an accelerative or decelerative force strong enough to operate the safety switch. The benefits of this device on a road car are obvious, but on the circuit where a little contact is par for the course this pesky little unit could take you out of the race. On my first dealing with such a device I removed the unit from the car (a Ferrari 360 Challenge) to work out the internal wiring with a multimeter. I was therefore rather surprised when one of my colleagues entered the workshop and started the car while I held the device in my hand. In this case the device did not break a circuit; it completed one that sent a signal to the ECU telling it to stop the fuel.

If you are lucky enough to have an inertia switch of this type then it is simply a matter of removing it to prevent it from causing mayhem. However, some types actually break a circuit, effectively removing the current feed to the pump or what ever. In these types we need to check the wiring diagram to see which wires enter the switch, and then permanently connect them together, bypassing it. Make sure this is a connection to the high standards we discussed in the previous chapters, if only because it would be really embarrassing for you to endure a retirement due to the failure of your wiring modification.

Another safety system which is usually removed from a competition car is the airbag. Drivers are increasingly using the HANS (head and neck restraint system) to reduce the danger of serious neck and head injury in the event of a crash. HANS is a system designed to hold the helmet during an accident, preventing it from moving the neck to unnatural angles. This is the closest race drivers get to whiplash protection, as

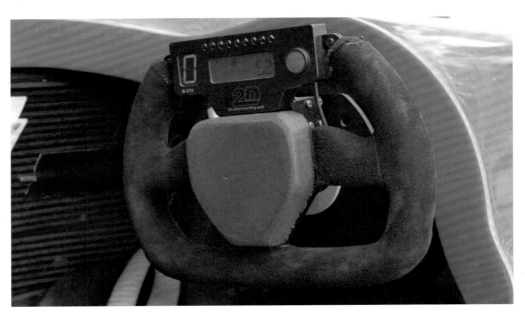

This system provides the driver with all the information he needs without having to peer into dark corners of the cockpit at various instruments. Note the inbuilt shift lighting. (Paul Martin)

This neat bit of design means that operating the fire extinguisher will also automatically kill the engine.

airbags rely on an inertia switch, which as mentioned before is not ideal for racing. Racing drivers also prefer to use smaller steering wheels to those fitted as standard, which gives us another reason for removing the standard-fit wheel. But what if that wheel is fitted with an airbag? Here is a basic guide to safe airbag removal, however bear in mind that this is just a generalised guide, and that airbags are dangerous. It is good practice to check with the manufacturer to ensure that you are not about to do something nasty to yourself.

Removing an airbag

The airbag usually consists of a unit mounted on the front face of the steering wheel. Before you do anything, disconnect the car battery. Once you have done this, look up the circuit diagram for the airbag. If it has a fuse (it might not) then pull this as well, just to be sure. Then go and have a cup of tea, mow the lawn – do anything, but don't do any further work on the car for at least half an hour, and make sure no-one else does anything on it either. You might like to turn on the ignition for a few seconds directly after disconnecting the battery just to make sure any residual current is dissipated.

After at least half an hour has passed you can start to remove the airbag assembly from the wheel. The techniques for doing this will vary from manufacturer to manufacturer, but normally consist of some Torx style screws accessed from the dashboard side of the wheel. Once these have been loosened the airbag unit will probably be ready to drop right into your hands. Simply pull the airbag away from the wheel, exposing the wiring beneath. Normally these plugs have special connectors

On a long race such as Le Mans the driver is stressed to the limit, increasing the risks in an already-dangerous sport. (Simon Crosse)

that short out the airbag terminals when there is no connector fitted. This reduces the chance of the airbag firing itself due to induced currents from other items nearby. Disconnect the plug, and put the airbag somewhere safe. Always store airbags with the side which normally faces the driver pointing up; if the airbag should set itself off it will do less damage this way. Don't just throw it in the bin as you could end up doing someone a great deal of harm on its journey between your garage and the landfill. If the removal of the airbag is to be a permanent modification then the wiring and actuation system can also be removed, assuming it doesn't interface with any other systems on the way.

When the driver is swamped with controls his workload and stress levels increase. It is standard practice to automate a fair number of controls, and despite modern domestic cars being more complicated under the skin than ever before, the process of driving remains unchanged, sometimes even simplified. For the domestic driver, small touches such as 'one-touch' closing of electric windows means the driver can return their attention to the road more rapidly, and thermostatic control of radiator fans and such mean that the driver often doesn't even know the system exists, let alone how important it is. The more systems we can automate in our competition car, the more we can allow the driver to get on with the driving.

The word *automation* comes from the Ancient Greek for *self-dictated*, which pretty well sums up what we are trying to achieve. With a high workload placed upon the driver his reaction times are likely to suffer, resulting in slower solutions to problems that occur. For example, we have discussed connecting the ignition through a failsafe circuit that kills the engine should oil pressure be lost; this system will operate a lot

It's even more important to clearly mark the kill switch when it is as small as this!

Every system that is automated is another problem removed from the driver.

quicker than the driver could. Lots of miniscule delays can add up to a large amount of time lost which could destroy an engine. The time taken for the bulb to illuminate, the time taken for the driver to acknowledge the warning lamp, the driver getting to a point where he has a hand free to operate the kill switch or ignition, all of these things take time. So sometimes we might automate a system purely because this way we can operate it more efficiently than the driver could.

Other times, automation helps us in different ways; a device called a turbo timer is fitted to highly tuned turbocharged cars to allow the engine to idle for a few minutes after the ignition switch has been turned off. This gives the turbo a proper opportunity to slow down, so that when the engine is finally allowed to turn off the turbocharger isn't spinning away on bearings which are now starved of oil. Continuing to run the engine prevents heat from building up in the turbocharger as it would if immediately stopped after high speed running. Both of these actions prolong the life of a very expensive component with no input from the driver.

It could be thought that all this automation is expensive, and in some situations it is; Keeping on the subject of a turbo timer, these units cost in excess of £100, and yet with very little electronics knowledge it is possible to construct a circuit using very few components, such as a 555 timer microchip, which will give us exactly the same result as a commercial system, at a fraction of the cost. With many systems automation is more a matter of a little applied ingenuity than spending a great deal of money.

Microswitches are miniature switches that are designed to be operated by cams or other mechanical input. These switches are very useful when trying to automate systems, as they can tell us when certain components are in particular positions. For example, if you wanted to limit the power in first gear to allow for better traction you could use a microswitch attached to the gear linkage. Some drivers like to have a light illuminate on the dash to tell them that they are achieving full throttle. Once this light appears the driver knows he does not need to bury the pedal any further as maximum

throttle opening has been achieved. A simple microswitch mounted on the throttle housing would accommodate this, linked to a lamp on the dashboard.

Toyota's first four-wheel-drive turbocharged Celica, the GT4 ST165 used a water-to-air intercooler to reduce the temperature of the inducted gases after pressurisation by the turbocharger. When the car detected that full throttle had been achieved a pump operated, flowing the dedicated intercooler coolant between the intercooler matrix and its radiator. Another application could be the monitoring of the brake and clutch pedals. On domestic cars fitted with cruise control microswitches are fitted to these pedals to disengage the system should the driver wish to regain control. On a racing car a microswitch on the clutch could inform the engine management that a momentary ignition cut is required to allow a full throttle gear change to take place.

Electronic systems use programmable logic devices (PLDs), to automate certain functions. A PLD can be programmed to look at a certain number of variables and take a certain action depending on the figures it has picked up. For example, a PLD can be used in a home-built shift light to decide that it will illuminate earlier when the engine is cold, to minimise damage. Scope for the application of PLDs is far too extensive to be covered in any real detail here, and there is a great deal of potential in these handy little devices.

OPPOSITE *This master switch does not just isolate the car electrics; it is designed to stop the engine as well. Note the lap timing sensor and data logger download connector.* (Paul Martin)

BELOW *Ergonomically this cockpit has been very well thought out, with everything within clear view and easy reach.*

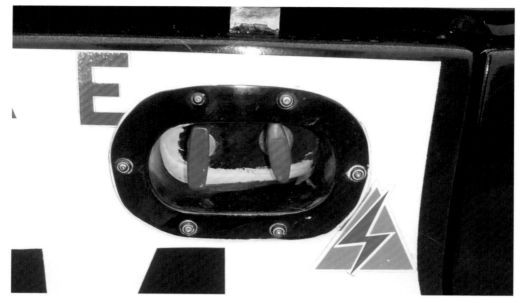

By recessing the emergency switches the risk of inadvertent operation can be minimised.

Neat cabling is less likely to chafe, and allows the scrutineers to do their job without needless clutter.

Whenever we build a control system based on variable inputs there are some things that have to be considered. The central heating system in your home uses a thermostat to switch the heating on and off as required. As the room heats up the thermostat switches off, turning off the heating. The temperature will then gently rise and fall about this point, maintaining consistent heat in the room. This is known as closed-loop feedback, as the variable being measured (the temperature) is directly affected by the system being switched on and off, forming a loop.

If you try turning your household thermostat back and forth over the switching point you will notice that the switch on and switch off points are not the same, and differ depending on which direction you are turning the thermostat control. This is to counteract an effect known as Hysteresis which is a term that broadly covers the speed at which our system reacts to a new input. Once the heating has come on in our centrally heated room the temperature change is not instant. In the same way, the room will continue to heat up after the heating has been switched off. Our thermostat takes this principle into account and switches off the heat slightly before the ideal temperature is reached. This gives the room time to settle in to its new temperature. If we didn't include this system the thermostat would go in to a condition known as 'hunting', where it keeps trying to reach the ideal temperature but goes too far either way each time.

You may be wondering what all this has to do with competition cars, but closed-loop systems on the vehicle have to operate in a similar fashion. ECU-controlled cooling fans have Hysteresis compensation built in, so the switch on and switch off points are not too close together. If they were at the same point then the fan would go on and off with little pause between each state. Starting a fan moving from stationary requires a lot more energy than maintaining it at one speed, so constantly switching it on and off as the temperature fluctuates minutely would be very wasteful. Building in a buffer zone of a few degrees is the electrical equivalent of incorporating some intentional 'slack in the linkage' to prevent the system from overcompensating.

If we look at a domestic car we can find a lot of automatic systems already in place. An automated system can be considered as simple as the courtesy light illuminating when you open the door, to being as complicated as a luxury car deciding that one side of the vehicle needs cooler air supplied to it due to the sun shining on that side. Obviously, the more complicated we allow things to become, the more chance there is of a component failure, and the more weight we have to carry around. Look at the switches you have on your dashboard; could you realistically automate any of these circuits? Does the driver *really* need to be able to control exactly which fuel pump is supplying the engine? A simple pressure switch could indicate that one fuel pump has failed, resulting in an instant changeover to the other. A warning lamp could inform the driver that this has taken place, but by the time he has registered the lamp the car has already removed the faulty component from the system. This sort of automation would not even require a PLD as some simple relay wiring would do the job.

The one thing that a driver can do which is harder for an automated system is to deal with is false alarms. Our circuit to kill the ignition upon loss of oil pressure seems a great idea, but what if the scavenge pipe on the oil pump momentarily comes out of the oil due to high cornering forces? As far as the engine is concerned the oil pressure has been lost, so the circuit cuts the ignition. A momentary problem which a driver would have acknowledged and dismissed is viewed as a critical emergency by our failsafe system, and could easily cost us the race. We could incorporate a delay system

OVERLEAF *Whilst safety regulations can be an irritation, it is nice to know that drivers are better protected now than they have ever been.* (Elliott Russell)

Apart from assisting with the set-up, a data logger can help point out where it all went wrong in the case of an accident.

that only kills the ignition if oil pressure is lost for a certain time, but now we are incorporating an intentional impediment into a system that was so valuable, primarily due to its rapid reaction time. These are the problems that we are required to face during the design of our automated controls. It is for this reason that it is advisable to include overrides that return control to the driver if needed. The disadvantage with this is that an override switch provides yet another switch in the cockpit, and wasn't the whole point of automation, to reduce the clutter in this area?

Chapter 11

In-car communication systems

Trying to make yourself heard in a competition car is rather like trying to put up a tent in a gale, only more frustrating. Mishearing pace notes can be rather expensive, so a high-fidelity communication (known as 'comms' or 'intercom') system is a prerequisite of any motorsport in which a co-driver or navigator is carried. Previously the cost of these systems was quite prohibitive, but as most amplifier circuits can now be mounted almost completely on one microchip the cost and size of in-car comms systems has been drastically reduced.

The other matter which has come about with the evolution of comms systems is a much lower current draw is now required. This means that an intercom can be fully powered by one or two 9V batteries, as found in domestic smoke alarms. This independence from the vehicle electrical system has a couple of advantages. First,

BELOW *A typical intercom connector.* (Peacemarsh Garage)

OVERLEAF *This crew are using boom mikes mounted to their helmets; ideally suited to this form of motorsport.* (Theunis du Plessis)

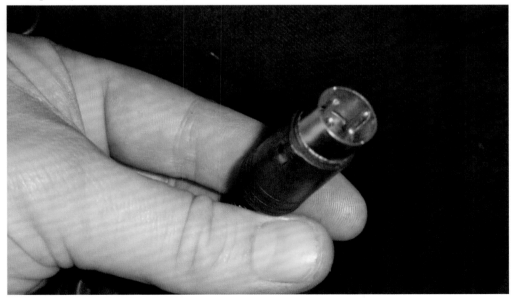

due to the power not being shared by the comms and ignition systems there is a reduction in the amount of interference transferred into the comms set-up. It also removes the requirement for the intercom to be wired to the main loom, meaning it can be mounted wherever is most convenient within the cockpit, and it means that the operation of the comms system is not dependent on the vehicle power being available.

Needless to say, if you don't want the worry of a flat battery then a system called a battery eliminator can be used, which will supply the correct voltage for the unit directly from the vehicle's 12V supply. An intercom system usually has speakers fitted within the crew's helmets, with a microphone incorporated on the front, or mounted on a boom in an open-face helmet. If there is no requirement to wear a helmet then a practice headset can be used, which is literally a pair of headphones fitted with a boom microphone. Volume control is usually fitted to the amplifier box itself, and can be set individually to suit each crew member's comfort.

The microphone is best placed so that the lips occasionally brush it in use, but if distortion or crackling is heard then the microphone is too close, although with modern systems this is unlikely to occur. Some systems allow you to adjust the sensitivity of the microphones, in which case, the distance between the microphone and the mouth becomes less critical. However, if we move the microphone away from the mouth and have to turn the sensitivity up to counteract the increased distance we are more likely to pick up surrounding noise, which is exactly what we should be trying to avoid. It is possible to purchase helmets in which the

In-car communications allow the driver and co-driver to clearly converse despite external distractions! (PIAA UK)

intercom components have already been installed. Those who have tried and failed when attempting to securely locate the earpieces in an off-the-shelf helmet will undoubtedly see the advantages of buying a system which already has these components fitted.

Usually, the in-car communication system is not the only form of comms available to the team. A radio set-up to communicate with the rest of the team can be fitted where regulations permit, enabling the driver to notify them of possible problems with the car to enable the service crew to be prepared in time for the vehicle's arrival at the pit, check on the progress of his nearest rivals, and so forth. Check the regulations with care as some events specifically ban radio systems to prevent communication that could interfere with the spirit of the event. The radio needs to be easily operable with the minimum of distraction to the cockpit crew as the more complicated the operation the less they are able to concentrate on the task in hand.

In aircraft, a simple PTT (push to transmit) button is placed under the pilot's trigger finger (don't believe Hollywood, that button is just the radio!). This means that once the radio has been set to the required frequency it is simply a matter of pressing the button to transmit the pilot's speech. It would not be terribly difficult to set the radio in a competition car to do exactly the same thing. Most teams using a PTT button mount it on the steering wheel to allow the driver to communicate with his service crew with the smallest drop in concentration possible. The radio systems usually interface with the in-car communications systems already discussed, keeping the duplication of equipment to a minimum.

The most obvious limitation with these systems is the range of the radio, but you can do your best to optimise this by mounting the aerial exactly as the manufacturer's guidelines suggest. These will vary, but usually require the aerial to be mounted on a metal panel, with excellent conductivity between the panel and the aerial base plate, preferably on an unpainted area. If the aerial lead supplied is already terminated then there is a pretty good chance that the cable length has been calculated to provide the most efficient conduction of radio energy possible and extending or shortening it could be detrimental to its abilities. Route the aerial and its cable away from other components if possible, and never place any of the components in the circuit anywhere near the ignition system or its components.

The further away the aerial and radio unit are placed from the ignition system the less chance there is of interference playing havoc with your reception and transmission. Keep all connections free from dirt and water, preferably by waterproofing them in some way. Obviously, we are limited in what we can do to waterproof a connector which is constantly being disconnected and reconnected, but one that is seldom separated can benefit from some cheap and simple waterproofing to improve reliability. A simple off-cut from a sandwich bag can be used to cover a connector and if tied in place with nylon tie-wraps water ingress can be minimised. Remember to fit the connector in such a way that if any water does enter it that it is visible, and therefore can be opened and cleaned before any real damage occurs.

In the old days equipment such as this was very susceptible to vibration, and needed to be mounted on anti-vibration mounts to keep it working. With the advent of solid state technology our equipment has become more and more rugged, resulting in these precautions becoming rather less important. However a lot of this kit is a big investment for smaller teams, and it is not unusual to see equipment such as this transferred between different cars as time goes on. Just because this kit is sturdier than it was a few years ago does not mean that it responds well to careless handling!

Sometimes the radio equipment is mounted in the footwell, perfectly placed to receive abuse from the co-driver's feet. The obvious solution with any equipment

ABOVE *A typical pit-to-car radio system.* (Elliott Russell)

OPPOSITE *Cable-ties are a quick and secure method of securing items in a competition car, in this example lap time sensors in a Ferrari 360 Challenge.* (Wren Classics)

placed in this area is to create a lightweight but sturdy cover to absorb some of these impacts. This is all well and good, but remember that certain types of high-power equipment are capable of generating quite a bit of heat which needs to be effectively dissipated from the unit to prevent failure. Leave an air gap around the unit to allow for this, but don't get carried away and encroach too far into the passenger cell. Remember also that you still need to be able to access all the buttons on the unit to operate it, and that you may need to see the various displays that it has. If any rotary knob on a unit such as this ever gets bent, assuming it still rotates, your best bet is to *not* to try to bend it back. If you do there is a pretty good chance you will end up with the knob broken off in your hand and a big bill for replacement. If it refuses to operate due to the bend then straighten it out just enough to get it working again and push it no further. It's one of those things that just has to be chalked up to experience.

Different countries have different laws regarding radio transmissions and just because a radio or frequency is legal in the UK does not mean you can use it on the continent, as it could be an emergency services frequency or reserved for other reasons. The event organisers should make it quite clear what equipment is allowed, and the frequencies with which it may be operated.

Radio equipment with a built-in aerial, such as a hand-held 'walkie-talkie' does not operate very well inside a vehicle. This is because the bodywork of the car acts like a 'Faraday Cage', and absorbs the majority of the RF signal before it reaches the handset. It is for this reason that the best reception is achieved by mounting the aerial on the bodywork of the vehicle. One of the most irritating factors of using a radio anywhere near a car is the interference caused by the ignition system, electric motors and myriad of other items seemingly designed to play havoc with the incoming signal.

There are a number of things that can be done to minimise this, the most important of which is to make sure the ignition system is putting out a minimum of RF energy. This can be done by having the radio unit and aerial well earthed to the bodywork. If the radio transceiver is metal cased then it may prove beneficial to mount an extra earth lead to it, to be sure of a good connection. For plastic-cased receivers a metal case mounted around it and grounded to the bodywork will almost certainly prove beneficial. Using good-quality co-axial cable for the aerial lead will certainly help, although the manufacturer is likely to have provided this anyway. Check all terminations and connectors are clean, and corrosion and moisture free.

Using a ferrite block on the power leads is likely to reduce RF from being transmitted along the power leads. Ferrite is a material consisting of various oxides, primarily iron oxide. When a cable is passed through a ferrite 'donut' then any RF the cable was radiating is absorbed by the ferrite and dissipated as heat. For such an application the amount of heat generated is not going to be noticeable, but just the presence of a ferrite RF inhibitor can clean up a lot of signal noise. Placing a capacitor across the 12V and earth terminals of the radio will help to smooth out any voltage spikes that might be generated by other equipment. Motors with dirty or pitted brushes are likely to produce small sparks and arcing that would normally cause no problems, but can appear as an annoying crackle on the radio. Cleaning the commutator and brush equipment is a good start towards reducing this interference, as is placing a small capacitor across the motor terminals. This will reduce the arcing and carries out exactly the same task as the archaically named condenser which was found under the distributor cap of older ignition systems.

Using high-contrast lettering to label the switchgear assists when trying to find a system control when under stress.

Using resistor spark plugs is also beneficial, as it reduces the RF noise generated by the spark crossing the plug gap. The original Land Rover was supplied to the Army in many variants, one of which was known as the FFR (Fitted For Radio). The FFR used 24V electrics rather than 12V, and had a number of different fitments to make using radios on board easier. However, the feature of most interest to us was the plug leads and ignition system. To ensure that the minimum RFI was generated by the system the plug leads had a wire mesh over-braid, designed to keep the radiation contained within the lead. (Plug leads are discussed in more depth in Chapter 7.)

If suffering from interference from a system other than the ignition then the easiest way to track down the culprit is to pull all of the circuit breakers or fuses and refit them one by one. As soon as the interference returns you can find out which items are fitted to the circuit you reinstated and their RFI resistance can be improved accordingly. As mentioned before, for most motors, fitting a small capacitor across the terminals is enough to improve matters. You may consider that some items are used so rarely that the RFI is not an issue although good practice dictates that all sources of interference should be eliminated if it is possible to do so.

Most of the controls on modern radios are fairly self explanatory; but the one system people ask about more than any other is 'squelch'. Many radios today have this controlled entirely electronically, so the operator does not need to worry about it and those which are fitted with it are very easy to understand. Squelch is a control designed to turn off the loudspeaker when a signal is not powerful enough to be considered usable; in other words, it silences the speaker unless someone tries to

This OMP-branded intercom system is simple to use, and has proven to be reliable in use. (Peacemarsh Garage)

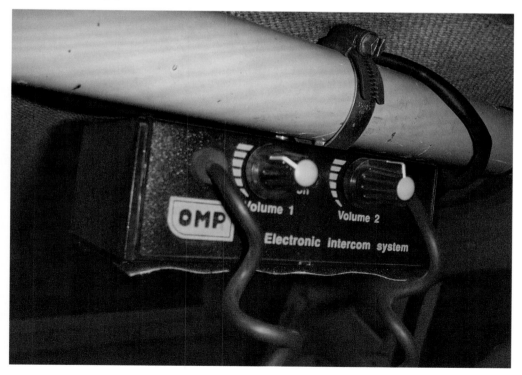

PREVIOUS PAGE *Every deflection of the suspension can be logged and used for refining settings.* (Paul Martin)

communicate with the listener. This means that in normal use the background static hiss is removed, allowing the listener to concentrate on other things.

Radios fitted with a knob marked 'Squelch' allow you to change the threshold at which the cut-off takes place. This is useful if you are trying to hear a weak signal, as you can turn down the threshold allowing it (and of course, the static) to be heard. For normal use the squelch control is turned up until the static noise cuts out, and if the occasional burst of static cuts through then a further tweak up can be made. Alternatively you can leave the control slightly lower than usual if you are expecting the incoming signal to be weak. If you turn the squelch up too high then you are likely to cut out the signal you are trying to receive, so care must be taken to get the setting right. For the ranges most radio systems use the squelch can be classed as one of those features that is 'set and forgotten'.

Some systems allow us to send telemetry back to a computer in the pits providing the ability to monitor the car in real time. This allows us to pick up feedback on a number of different parameters that may be monitored by data logging equipment on the car. Typically, a telemetry system would give feedback on oil pressure, engine speed and accelerative forces, to name just a few of the possibilities.

During testing many more parameters might be measured, such as the measurement of suspension displacement by utilising devices known as LDVTs (Linear Variable Displacement Transformers). These are devices used for giving an electrical output depending on the position of the shaft. Looking a little like a small hydraulic ram, these devices can be attached to suspension components to record how they move during use. They have a few very important advantages over using a potentiometer: they are practically infinite in the minuteness of the changes they can register: they are lightweight; have very little friction (which in turn gives them a long life), and they are also very accurate. Although they are more expensive than their potentiometer equivalents, this is offset by their much greater reliability and longer life (due to there being no wearing parts within the unit). Any device that measures something and then feeds a variable based on that measurement to a recording or display system is called a transducer.

Transducers can be anything from a temperature sender to a fuel quantity sender unit, and anything that can be displayed on the dashboard is capable of being sent via telemetry back to the pits. How often this data is recorded depends on a parameter called the sampling rate. For example, if we wanted to measure and record the temperature of the track surface then we could do this every half hour without missing much. If we were to measure this data every second then we would become swamped with thousands of practically identical figures which were largely superfluous.

Measuring the oil pressure during cornering in our competition car however, requires a very fast sample rate to ensure that no important data is missed. Thus we can see the importance of finding the right sample rate to suit the parameter we are trying to measure. Sample rates are normally measured in Hz, for example, the engine speed might be recorded at 10Hz, or ten times a second.

There is also the possibility of providing two-way telemetry. This means that instead of the pit crew just being provided with the data they can actually act upon it, conceivably meaning that adjustments such as fuel mixture and ignition timing can be tweaked mid-race. As around 50 channels can be monitored by most telemetry systems, including air pressure sensors, to give feedback on the aerodynamics of the car, the potential for tweaking and tuning the engine and chassis is huge, which give a welcome advantage in this highly competitive field.

Glossary of terms and abbreviations

Many of the terms listed here may have a different meaning in different environments; I have only listed meanings directly relating to this book.

Alternating current A voltage supply which alternates between positive and negative values, usually at a fixed speed and with zero volts as a reference. For example, UK domestic electricity is supplied at 240Vac, 50Hz, the voltage cycles 50 times a second.

Alternator The modern equivalent of a dynamo, an alternator supplies AC current, which is normally rectified and regulated on board the unit to provide a dc output usable by the vehicle electrics. It is usually belt-driven from the front pulley of the engine.

Alumina One of the constituents of the insulating material found in spark plugs.

Ammeter A device to measure current; fitted in series with the item to be tested in the electrical circuit. Measurements carried out in amperes, often shortened to amps.

Ampere Defined as 1 coulomb per second flowing in a circuit. It is a measurement of current in a circuit, similar to a measurement of rate of flow in a hydraulic system. It is given the symbol A.

Amp hour A rating given to a battery to define how much current the battery can supply over a given time.

Analogue Analogue data is infinitely variable, such as water temperature.

Armature Part of an electromagnetic device designed to move when current is applied.

Ballast resistor A component inserted in a circuit to compensate for changes. One is required when using an **LED** as a cockpit indicator, and in certain ignition systems.

Battery An array of cells designed to supply direct current by converting stored chemical energy into electrical energy.

Bimetal A short length of two different metals, bonded together. When heat is applied (or a current resulting in heat) the two metals expand at different rates, causing the strip to bend. This bending can be used to operate a switch or move a needle on a gauge.

Bimetallic gauge An instrument using the properties of a bimetallic strip to move a needle, giving a visual indication of a quantitative measurement.

Candela The unit of luminous power, sometimes referred to as candle power.

Capacitor A component designed to store an electric charge.

Capacitor discharge ignition An ignition system utilising a capacitor to create a high voltage burst of current to drive the primary winding of the ignition coil.

Carburettor A device to mix air and fuel in the correct ratio for combustion before being ingested by the engine, usurped by more precise, but more complicated fuel injection in most race engines.

Catalytic converter A device placed in the exhaust system of modern production cars to convert waste gases into chemicals slightly less damaging to the environment. Most racing cars dispense with this unit, however some classes of racing insist that the system remains in situ.

Closed-loop control A system that adjusts itself according to feedback from system output. Fuel injection can be closed-loop if a Lambda sensor is included to monitor the unburnt oxygen content of the exhaust gases. From this information adjustments are automatically carried out to correct the mixture to its Stoichiometric ideal.

Coil ignition A system using the collapse of an electrical field around a coil to produce a high-voltage spark.

Combustion chamber The part of an engine where the fuel/air mixture is burnt to produce pressure and therefore power.

Commutator A segmented slip ring arrangement designed to maintain power to the coils of a motor or dynamo in the required polarity.

Conductor A material that can carry electric current.

Connector A device for coupling two or more cables, or to provide an easy disconnection point.

Contact breaker See **Points**.

Circuit breaker A protection device fitted just after the power supply of a circuit designed to 'trip', or disconnect, current from a system in the event of an overload. Unlike a fuse it is capable of being reset and used again. Usually referred to as a 'CB'.

Coulomb A unit of electricity equal to the amount of charge flowed by a current of one amp in one second. If it could be compared to a hydraulic quantity then it could be considered similar to a gallon; in other words, a quantity. It is given the symbol C, but is rarely used in everyday electrical work.

Crankshaft sensor A sensor used by the ignition/fuel injection system to determine the position of the crankshaft. This allows the ECU to decide when the fuelling and spark ignition should take place.

Crimping A form of termination that securely attaches a terminal to a cable. Many people in motorsport do not like crimping, believing it to be less secure than soldering. However, it is the primary form of termination in the aviation industry.

Current The flow of electricity through a conductor, such as a cable.

Delta configuration One possible arrangement of the field coils in an alternator. The other possible arrangement is Star configuration. Delta configuration is so called because the coils are connected in a triangular pattern.

Detonation Also known as 'pinking', detonation is the combustion of the air/fuel mixture before it is required, resulting in a loss of power and possible engine damage.

Digital Digital data varies in steps. For example, an oil pressure gauge is analogue because it gives an infinitely variable quantitative measurement, whereas an oil pressure lamp is either on or off; it has two modes of operation and is therefore digital.

Dim-dip A system fitted to vehicles to ensure that when sidelights were selected, the vehicle's headlight filaments illuminated at a reduced intensity.

Diode A device that allows current to flow in one direction only.

Direct current A voltage supply which does not cycle in the way that alternating current does. For example, a smoke alarm battery supplies 9Vdc, a fixed nine volts.

Distributor A device fitted to cars without engine management to divert the spark produced by the coil to the cylinder that requires it.

Distributorless ignition An ignition system that is not reliant on a distributor to divert the spark to the required cylinder. See also **Twin coil ignition**.

Dry battery A battery made up of dry cells, also known as a Leclanché battery, after its inventor, Georges Leclanché. An example of a dry battery can be found in most torches, portable radios and smoke alarms.

Dwell The percentage of time that a contact breaker remains closed with relation to the rotation of the cam that actuates it. Can also be expressed as a percentage.

Dynamo The forerunner of the **Alternator** which provides dc current without the need for rectification due to its use of a **Commutator**. Generally, not as powerful as an *alternator* of similar size.

Earth An electrical connection to the bodywork usually linked to the negative terminal of the battery. By using the bodywork as a return for the electrical circuit the amount of wiring the vehicle has to carry is reduced.

ECU Electronic control unit, the 'brains' of the fuel injection/ignition system.

Electromagnet A magnet that consists of a metallic core (usually iron) that can have its magnetism switched on or off by the application of current to a coil wrapped around it.

Electronic ignition Ignition that is controlled electronically, as opposed to being initiated by a contact breaker system.

Engine management The electronic control of the engine systems, obtaining feedback from various sensors placed around the engine.

Fast charging Charging a battery rapidly utilising a special charger designed for the purpose.

Filament The more accurate term for a 'bulb'. The term filament refers to the slender wire suspended within a vacuum inside the glass bulb, which when current is applied will glow due to its highly resistive nature.

Fuel injection system A system for injecting precisely measured quantities of fuel into the engine to provide the correct ratio fuel/air mix for efficient combustion. The modern equivalent of the **Carburettor**.

Fuse A small strip of metal designed to melt if too much current is drawn over it. It is a sacrificial weak link to protect electrical equipment and is used extensively on production cars due to low cost, but is increasingly replaced by **Circuit breakers** on competition vehicles.

Hall effect ignition An ignition system triggering based upon a magnetic field being interrupted by a metallic object, in this case a 'chopper' on the shaft of the distributor.

Halogen lighting Halogen is a gas used to surround the filament in a bulb.

Hot wire sensor Calculates the quantity of air flowing through an induction system, basing its measurements on the cooling properties of the air as it passes over the element.

Hydrocarbons Chemicals present in exhaust fumes, containing only hydrogen and carbon atoms.

Ignition A system for introducing a spark to the combustion chamber of an internal combustion engine to ignite the fuel/air mix.

Indirect injection The most common form of fuel injection, where the fuel is fed into the inlet manifold, as opposed to a direct injection system, as found in diesels and some of the latest petrol injection systems.

Injector A device for squirting fuel under high pressure into the inlet manifold or combustion chamber.

Insulator A material that cannot carry electrical current.

Interference An unwanted signal that interferes with other electronic devices.

Intermittent fault A fault which only occurs occasionally, making diagnosis difficult.

Inverter A device for converting dc into ac.

Instrument voltage stabiliser A device for supplying instruments which require a stable voltage.

Joule The unit of energy or work, equal to the work done when an object with an applied one Newton of force moves one metre in the direction of application.

Lambda The eleventh letter of the Greek alphabet, referring to the ideal ratio of fuel to air, also called the Stoichiometric Ratio. Usually a **Stoichiometric ratio** of 1 is considered to be 14.7:1 fuel to air.

Lambda sensor A sensor designed to measure the unburnt oxygen present in exhaust gases. This information is fed back to the fuel injection system so that the ECU can make fuelling adjustments to maintain the correct fuel/air mixture.

LCD Liquid crystal display; a device utilising a liquid which polarises its crystals when electricity is applied. When used in conjunction with polarised glass or transparent plastic, a section of the display will appear blacked out. When organised into sections or segments, an LCD display can give a read out of figures or symbols.

Lead/acid battery A battery consisting of lead plates with a dilute sulphuric acid electrolyte, commonly used in production cars. Calcium is added sometimes to the lead during manufacture, which reduces the amount of gas produced while charging, which allows the battery to be sealed permanently (known generically as 'Maintenance-free').

LED LED is an acronym of light emitting diode, a small semiconductor device which emits light when supplied with correct polarity current flow. In all other respects it acts in exactly the same way as a diode.

Magnetic field An area around a magnetised object (or circuit carrying current) in which a magnetic force can be detected.

Magneto A device found on smaller, usually older engines that uses permanent magnets to generate a spark for ignition purposes. Relatively obsolete in the face of coil-fed ignition systems.

Mapped ignition A form of electronic ignition which uses a chart of two or three dimensions (or 'map') to decide what timing/fuelling the engine should run, dependent on the variables fed to it by its sensors.

Momentary switch A switch which only remains closed while force is applied to the operating lever/button.

Motor An electrical device relying on the principle of electromagnets to convert electrical energy into a rotational force.

Moving coil instrument A gauge that uses a magnetic coil used in conjunction with a permanent magnet to convert a current input into the movement of a needle, to provide a visual representation of a quantitative measurement. Works in a similar fashion to the **Moving iron instrument**.

Moving iron instrument A gauge working in a similar fashion to a moving-coil instrument, except that the coil is fixed, and the needle is attached to an iron armature.

Multiplex The process of transmitting two or more signals simultaneously along a single transmission line.

Multi-point injection A fuel injection system utilising more than one injector, usually one per cylinder.

Ohm A unit of electrical resistance, represented by the symbol Omega. One ohm is equal to the resistance between two points on a conductive material when a potential difference of one volt produces a current of one amp.

Ohms Law The physical law first expressed by Georg Simon Ohm, who stated that current increases in direct proportion to the voltage supplied.

Oil pressure switch A switch that closes a circuit when the oil pressure supplied to it drops below a preset level. Usually used to operate a warning lamp.

Parallel A form of circuit connection in which the components are connected with a common input and a common output, as opposed to in series, where the output of one component is connected to the input of the next

Points A device usually situated in the distributor of older engines, which is timed to supply and disconnect the power to the primary winding of the ignition coil in a manner which causes the coil to produce a spark when it is required to do so.

PCB A printed circuit board, is a board to which electronic components are soldered. The board is coated with copper, which is etched away in certain places using acid. This leaves a circuit to which the components can be mounted to form a circuit. PCBs are often used in instrument clusters on modern production cars, as it is quick and simple to wire the instruments using this technique.

Rectifier The opposite of an **Inverter**, a rectifier takes ac and turns it into something approaching dc. Usually, the output of a rectifier will need some extra adjustment to turn it into true dc.

Reed switch A switch which either opens or closes depending on its proximity to a magnetic field.

Regulator A device for maintaining current or voltage at a preset level.

Relay A switch controlled by an electromagnet, often used for the control of high-current circuits.

Resistance The restriction that a material presents to the flow of electrical current through it, measured in ohms.

Sampling rate The amount of times a recording device takes a reading of the value it is measuring, usually in Hz (times per second).

Schmitt trigger An electronic circuit that gives an output when the input exceeds a preset threshold level. It usually utilises two transistors, one of which feeds its output signal back to the first, resulting in rapid switching. Often used in electronic ignition systems.

Scotch-lok connector A connector created to form a temporary connection or addition to a wiring loom. Not used in competition cars.

Sealed beam A type of headlight where the entire headlight and reflector assembly forms the bulb. Basically the entire light unit is a sealed bulb, which is entirely replaced in the event of a filament failure.

Shift light A lamp which illuminates at or near the maximum RPM of the engine to tell the driver to change gear.

Single-point injection A type of fuel injection utilising a single injector at a common point to all cylinders on the intake manifold. Primarily used on smaller-engined economy models, it is gradually being phased out in favour of **Multi-point injection** systems.

Solder Low-melting point metal which is melted with a soldering iron to create an electrically conductive joint between two wires, a wire and a component or a component and a circuit board. (Traditional lead-based solder is soon to be banned from sale in the UK due to health and safety legislation.)

Solenoid A high-current relay, used for switching the current supply to the starter motor. Also a term used to describe an electromagnetic device which moves an armature when current is applied. Solenoids are used in items such as central locking motors and electric boot release systems.

Spark plug A component which protrudes into the combustion chamber to carry the spark produced by the ignition system.

Speedometer An instrument which informs the driver how fast the vehicle is travelling.

Star configuration One possible arrangement of the field coils in an alternator. The other is Delta configuration. Star configuration is so called because the coils are connected in a centrally converging pattern, visually similar to a star.

Starter motor Designed to spin the crankshaft of the engine up to a speed at which the combustion process will start and the engine will then sustain its own rotation.

Stepper motor A type of motor which gives a very precise output as it has more poles than a normal motor. This also gives it a great deal of torque for its size. Stepper motors are often used in high-quality **Tachometers** due to their accuracy and resistance to movement by external forces.

Stoichiometric ratio The ideal ratio of air to fuel, usually considered to be 14.7:1 by mass.

Suppression The prevention of electrical interference from one system to another.

Tachometer An instrument that informs the driver of the engine speed. Usually fed from the ignition system or ECU.

Thermistor A semiconductor which changes its resistance depending on the temperature applied to it. Used in thermostatic temperature control and instrumentation.

Thermocouple A temperature sensor consisting of a junction of two different metals, which, when heated produces a small voltage. Usually requires a control unit to give an output that can be monitored on a gauge.

Toggle switch A switch which has two positions, and when operated will remain in the position selected.

Transistor To oversimplify, a transistor is the semiconductor equivalent of a relay, but capable of finer control than merely on or off. Used in most amplification devices and found in virtually every electronic system.

Trigger level The threshold at which a circuit is activated.

Vacuum advance Automatic adjustment of ignition timing, carried out by using the vacuum created in the inlet manifold to operate a sensor, or in older engines, rotate the contact breaker assembly to advance or retard the timing.

Volt A unit of measurement that defines the potential difference between two points in a circuit. Sometimes this difference is referred to as electromotive force (EMF). If equated to a hydraulic system, the volt could be considered similar to psi as a unit of pressure or force. A battery can be said to have a voltage of 12V, in other words a potential difference of twelve volts between the positive and negative battery terminals. The universal symbol for voltage is V.

Voltage regulator A device for maintaining a voltage at a preset level. Often used to create a stable voltage supply to improve the accuracy of instrumentation.

Voltmeter An instrument which indicates the voltage over two points, such as the terminals of a battery.

Warning lamp A light which illuminates to bring a problem to the attention of the driver.

Watt A unit of power equal to the power produced by a current of one amp acting across a potential difference of one volt. The watt is the rate of energy being utilised, in joules per second. For example, a car headlamp bulb may have a power rating of 55W. It is universally recognised by the symbol W.

Wheatstone bridge A circuit consisting of three known resistances (one of which can usually be varied) and an unknown resistance (such as a **Thermistor**). By adjusting the variable resistance until the galvanometer (a type of sensitive voltmeter) reads zero, the resistance of the unknown component can be found.

Zener diode A type of semiconductor used as a voltage regulator.

Zirconium dioxide An element used in the construction of a **Lambda sensor**.

Index